If I can, you can

The biography of Hayden Walsh

Karen O'Sullivan

Published by **in case of emergency press** 2022

Copyright © Karen O'Sullivan 2022

All rights reserved. Without limiting the rights under copyright reserved above, no part of this publication may be reproduced, stored in or introduced into a database and retrieval system or transmitted in any form or any means (electronic, mechanical, photocopying, recording or otherwise) without the prior written permission of both the owner of copyright and the above publishers.

ISBN 978-0-6451280-9-3

Cover photograph: Carl Morris

in case of emergency press

We are proud to acknowledge the Traditional Owners of country throughout Australia and to recognise their continuing connection to land, waters, and culture.
We pay our respects to their Elders.
We support recognition, reconciliation, and reparation.

For Yessah and Shanaya

Table of contents

Foreword	i
Chapter One	1
Chapter Two	19
Chapter Three	37
Chapter Four	49
Chapter Five	66
Chapter Six	80
Chapter Seven	96
Chapter Eight	107
Chapter Nine	127
Chapter Ten	142
Chapter Eleven	154
Chapter Twelve	172
Acknowledgements	185
About the Author	187

If I can, you can

The biography of Hayden Walsh

by Karen O'Sullivan

Foreword

Nathan Buckley

Success is being able to live life on your own terms which, as I understand it, is not an encouragement to live selfishly but an encapsulation of the idea that we all possess gifts of one description or another and with them we must create for ourselves a life of unique expression.

Basically, if life is a song how will we sing it?

By this definition, few people I have encountered across my years have succeeded in the way Hayden Walsh has.

It seems to me that Hayden has defined himself or, perhaps, refused to define himself, in a way unexpected and allowed his joyous, unshackled thinking to take him beyond the expectations of his circumstances.

We first met over 20 years ago, in a ward of the Royal Children's Hospital, as Hayden was preparing for an operation. Our paths have crossed intermittently since; on a football field late in my playing career as I was coming to terms with my sporting mortality and, more recently, on the occasion of Hayden's 28th birthday.

He is a friend to many at Collingwood—Jarryd Blair and Jordan De Goey in particular—and for good reason. Hayden is passionate and warm and in possession of a sense of humour that comes at you from unexpected angles. His lack of guile can open a wonder in those he connects with. He is filled, like a Santa sack, with dreams and possibilities.

If I can, you can

With braces on both legs, Hayden kicked the football for 20 minutes with Jordan after a training session in 2019. It was hard to know who was happier.

In the same year Hayden's partner gave birth to their baby. It was told to me that not since 1995, when Hayden's beloved Kyneton Tigers broke a 29-year premiership drought, had as many smiles been seen in his hometown. I can believe the story.

A triumph of will, a celebration of determination and an inspiring example of thinking without limits are the chords of Hayden's tune.

I have been fortunate to meet him.

Nathan Buckley
Former Collingwood Football Club coach, player and 2011 AFL Hall of Fame

Chapter One

I was 27 years old, approaching my twenty-eighth birthday and feeling miserable. Something was missing in my life. Although I had a smile better than his, and was obviously taller, I didn't look or move like Hollywood actor Tom Cruise. But I wanted that feeling he got after meeting and falling in love with fellow actor Katie Holmes. Cruise famously announced his newfound love to the world while jumping up and down on talk show host Oprah Winfrey's couch. He was deliriously happy, and that's what I wanted; to be deliriously happy and in love. I wasn't lonely all of the time, just some of the time. I had lots of friends, work colleagues and a loving family, as well as my trusty Fox Terrier, Bella. It may sound corny, but it was as simple as this: I was looking for love.

Some of my friends were happy in long-term relationships and my best mate had just got engaged. So, I felt that it was time for me to take the plunge and find that special person who could fulfil my dream to have my own family, my own home and live happily ever after. A prince, waiting for his princess sort of thing. I wanted someone to complete me, just like Beyonce completed Jay Z, Victoria completed David Beckham and Linda completed Paul McCartney.

The problem was, I wasn't a hunky movie star, a famous singer or elite sportsman, and to complicate things further, I lived with a disability. But as you will soon learn, I have never been one to let my physical imperfections get in the way of my progress. So, I set about my journey to find love with all the vigour of a reality TV 'Survivor' contestant competing for the million-dollar first prize. I wasn't leaving this Island!

It was 2018 and I was living in my family home with my parents in the regional Victorian town of Kyneton, about 90 kilometres north-west of Melbourne, with a reasonably small population where everybody knew everybody. I hadn't found my perfect match in almost 28 years, and I wasn't prepared to sit around and wait any longer for Miss Right to come along. I knew that I had to go further afield to find her. So, enter online dating, the perfect platform for me to cast my net in search of love.

I had lived my entire life with Mum and Dad, and I had no siblings, so it had always been just the three of us. The first home I remember was a weatherboard, before we upgraded to a brick house just up the road. Kyneton was considered a charming old town that was settled in the mid-1800's and was considered a gateway and supply centre to the Goldfields of Bendigo, Clunes and Castlemaine. Its history is reflected through the trademark bluestone buildings and cobblestone pathways that line Piper Street, now a bustling weekend destination for foodies and city-dwellers eager to leave the rat-race behind.

One afternoon as I sat at my desk, staring out of my bedroom window into our backyard, I opened my laptop and began setting up my personal 'eHarmony' profile. Answering all 32 of the online questions required a level of honesty that most people would never need to consider, or might simply be too afraid to divulge. It wasn't just information like the colour of my hair, eyes and other common features that I needed to include. My personal details had to go to the next level. Living with a disability meant that I had to take a huge leap of faith by sharing this personal information with prospective partners and cross my fingers it would pay off. I wanted to find love just as much as other people my age. But, like all things I wanted, I had to go about getting them differently—my own way. So, I took a warts-and-all approach, filling in the required fields and uploading several photos. I chose what I thought were snaps which reflected my happy and cheery nature and my cheeky smile (better than Tom's) but I also included photos that clearly highlighted my less-than-perfect stature. There were no secrets or surprises; my profile spelled out the fact that I had been born with a disability that I would live with for the rest of my life.

Cerebral palsy, also known as CP, is the most common disability in children and, on average, an Australian child is born with CP every 15 minutes. In most cases the disability is caused during pregnancy when the developing brain is somehow damaged. In a small number of cases a child can develop CP during birth if their brain is deprived of oxygen for a long period of time. CP is a lifelong disability and there is no cure as yet. Children with CP can be diagnosed with anything from a mild form, where they are relatively 'able', to an extreme case where 24-hour care is required.

My CP was mild but still caused my leg muscles to be extremely tight, affecting my mobility and resulting in a permanent limp on my right side. I wore lower leg ankle and foot orthotics (known as AFO's and often referred to as callipers or splints) which were made from a hard plastic that wrapped around the top of my calves then extended down the back of my lower legs and under my feet. My splints supported my weak calf muscles and were intended to keep my feet straight and help me walk, preventing my limp from getting worse. After I'd been on my feet for a few hours, the splints felt tight and painful, and the only way I could find relief was to take them off and have a hot bath or shower. I used metal sticks that helped me stand and walk and my hands were also affected with tightening of some of the muscles in my fingers, causing them to bend the wrong way. Some people even asked me if I had arthritis in my fingers because they looked like they'd been crushed! I'd sometimes reply, 'You should see the other guy!'. Also, my speech was slow and slurred. But don't be fooled, I was just as switched on as the next bloke! CP is not a genetic condition and exactly why I was born with it remains unclear. But most importantly, I felt that my abilities far outweighed my disability!

So, sitting in front of my computer that morning in early 2018, I truthfully told eHarmony all of the things I could do, like drive a car, go to work and play football. Of course, I was very hopeful that the photos of my perfect teeth and beaming smile would be enough to woo the women, but I also felt deeply that if someone wanted to get to know me, and hopefully grow to love me, they had to accept everything about me, splints and all.

Feeling totally vulnerable and nervous, I wondered whether any women would take the time to read through my profile and learn about me, including my disability. Would any of them take up the opportunity to get to know me, or would they exit my profile when they saw that I lived with CP?

A dark voice in my head tried to convince me that nobody would ever want me. Who would choose to love a disabled man with many more needs than ordinary, able-bodied men? But plenty of people loved their preloved, sometimes dinted cars, right? So, I thought, if there was a market for second-hand vehicles, surely there'd be somebody who would love a man with a limp and a killer smile. I also wondered about the sort of partner I would want to connect with. Would I consider someone if she also lived with a disability or not? I was excited and nervous at the same time, but mostly hoping that my loneliness would end and be replaced with a kind, caring partner.

With a steely resolve and determination to continue my online search for friendship, companionship and possibly love, I looked at myself in the mirror and made a pact with myself not to give up. I was ready for intimacy, and nothing was going to stop my endeavours to fulfil my dreams. Challenge accepted other Survivor contestants— I'll see you at the finish.

You see, this wasn't my first foray into online dating. A few years earlier I'd dabbled with this modern way of finding friendship and met up with a couple of women, the first when I was 24.

Lisa, who was also 24, lived in another regional town on the other side of the city; so we chose to meet up in Melbourne for dinner. Unlike our online conversations, which had been interesting and promising, our meeting was not. But I had made one big mistake back then, I had been too scared to mention in my profile that I lived with a disability. I wanted to be judged for the person I was, not my disability. Lisa only discovered I had cerebral palsy when I limped nervously into the pub to have dinner with her. Then when I reached out to greet her with a hug, anyone would have thought that I had an infectious disease the way she stepped back quickly, away from my embrace. I almost fell forward with only my sticks keeping me upright, which was a disastrous beginning to what I'm sure was the fastest counter meal eaten in the history of mankind. Lisa tried to make conversation, asking me about my disability, but I felt so embarrassed, I quickly scoffed down my chicken parma, chips and salad and left with my tail between my crooked legs.

I felt utterly devastated and rejected after my first online date, and wiped Lisa's profile from my eHarmony account in an attempt to erase what was an epic fail.

Still yearning to share my life with someone special, it took me about 12 months to work up the courage to try the process again and I was matched with a woman in Canberra named Zoe. This time, I had accepted that I must be honest and brave, and included my disability in my profile, so there were no surprises and Zoe knew exactly what she was in for. Canberra is about seven hours north of Kyneton, but as I hadn't been matched with anybody closer to home, I decided to get in touch with her and see how we got on. The early signs were great; she loved Australian rules football like me, even though she barracked for the Sydney Swans and I was a one-eyed Collingwood supporter. As if having CP wasn't enough!

After just a few weeks of chatting online she was keen to meet me and invited me to Canberra for a weekend. My parents were not over the moon about the idea of me going by myself, so the three of us went on the seven-hour road trip to meet this potential new partner. It was a great weekend and Zoe was lovely. We talked non-stop for two days and seemed to have a lot in common and, importantly, my CP didn't appear to be a problem for her. We went to the movies, the sports museum and also indulged in her love of retail therapy, then later met up with my parents for dinner.

I thought everything had gone smoothly, but to my surprise and utter disappointment, I was wrong. Soon after my return home she sent me a message saying that she was sorry, but she just wanted to be friends, then she blocked me on eHarmony. Huh! Some friend! The all too familiar feeling of devastation returned, and I thought, 'Here we go again'. As the grey cloud of loneliness sat familiarly upon my shoulders, I began to believe that there was no one out there for me at all.

Throughout my life my parents had always been there to support me during both the happy times and the sad times, of which there were many. However, this time was different; I was no longer a young boy. I was a man and the thought was crushing that no woman could ever love me for who I was.

My close friends were very supportive and took me to the footy and out for dinners and beers, but I knew that the only one who could really deal with the personal rejection was me.

I gave up on my online dating endeavours for a while and went about my life working, attending physiotherapy sessions, volunteering at Kyneton's local Football Netball Club, and filling my days in a way that masked my sense of isolation and loneliness.

Following those two failed online experiences, it took another 12 months before I was ready to try the whole thing again and returned to the whirlwind world of online dating. Third time's a charm?

So, by January 2018, having built up the courage required, I decided to reactivate my eHarmony account, tweaking it to include more about myself and more about my disability. Apart from being another year older and, I hoped, wiser, nothing had changed, nor had my feeling of longing for a relationship and a partner. I chose not to tell my parents about this as they feared another serious rejection might cause a repeat of what had happened eleven years earlier when my broken heart landed me in a psychiatric ward. So, for now, my re-energised journey to find love would remain a secret. As Tom Cruise plays in the movies, "your mission should you choose to accept it …"

After a few days of feeling nervous, vulnerable and anxious, eHarmony eventually replied, sending me the profiles of just a few women who, through their complex set of algorithms, it had determined I was most compatible with. I began carefully assessing the profiles and while there weren't many to choose from, I knew this time around I wanted to get it right. I'd already been hurt too many times.

I couldn't explain why, but after reading the first couple of profiles I got a gut feeling that those women weren't for me. Then, just like receiving an unopened giftbox, I stumbled across a profile I couldn't resist opening up and examining further.

This woman was mysterious from the beginning. She had a name I had never heard before and had no idea how to pronounce, and she was from Mauritius, a country I was also unfamiliar with (for some reason, I hadn't ever pictured myself being with a girl from a tropical island before). Her name was Yessah and she had a beautiful face, a lovely, olive complexion, stunning brown eyes and a smile that melted my heart. There was something about her that I felt an instant connection with. I clicked the 'like' button on her profile and sat tight, hoping that she, too, would follow suit and choose my profile which would give us the green light to connect.

For the next 24 hours, my wobbly legs anxiously carried me back and forth to my computer, hoping that Yessah liked what I had so honestly shared with the eHarmony world. It seemed like I had walked a marathon, but that's because each of my steps counts as 1.5 of yours (another mild CP superpower). I stared at the photos on her page; she was smiling at the camera while enjoying the sunshine at the beach with her sister. I felt as though she was looking straight at me. Would we ever get the chance to gaze into each other's eyes for real?

To my great joy and surprise, I actually didn't have to wait too long because the very next day Yessah replied—she wanted to connect with me! As if a dream had come true, Yessah had swiped right and we moved to the next level of contact by chatting in the online dating world!

With my two index fingers, I carefully and painstakingly typed my replies to Yessah's questions about my disability, my dog, my life. For the first time ever, I spelled out my whole existence to a complete stranger who was fast becoming my most intimate of confidantes.

However, there was still the niggling question of, "Why me?" hanging over my head. Why would she choose me as a person of interest, instead of an able-bodied man? Could I ever be enough for her? Did she consider me attractive? These worrying thoughts sat deeply in my mind, intent on disrupting my search for happiness.

But, once again, my determination to find love was strong enough for me to push these doubts aside and begin getting to know this incredible woman.

Yessah is pronounced, 'Yess-ah', and she was living in an outer Melbourne suburban area, about 100 kilometres south-east of Kyneton. Her profile included so many common interests that helped make us compatible: we both loved dogs, the beach and the sunshine. Before her arrival in Australia the previous year, Yessah had worked as a karate instructor in Mauritius which included teaching disabled children. I wondered whether her experience there had helped connect us. Was 'disabled' the magic word identified by eHarmony, the invisible string that drew us together?

Once we connected online, our friendship grew rapidly. We shared our mobile phone numbers and began texting so regularly that my two thumbs began to feel arthritic! Compared to my two-finger typing, this is an improvement, trust me. Then we progressed to the old-fashioned way of actually talking to each other on the phone, and then to FaceTiming. My parents knew something was going on as my $79-a-month mobile plan went out the window very quickly, much to Mum's dismay, and I recall Dad's words of wisdom, "Son, be very careful that you don't get heartbroken again. Be sure you get to know her before you bring her home and don't do anything silly!" Dad told me he couldn't bear seeing me go through more heartbreak, reminding me again of my stint in hospital after my failed teenage romance in year ten. (More about this later in the book!)

After just a few weeks Yessah asked me if I would like to meet up with her in Melbourne. Of course, I said yes and was so excited to be finally getting to meet her in person, although I felt extremely nervous, like the feeling you get when you line up to ride a rollercoaster. I felt sick with worry that, like the others, she would reject me after meeting me. But I was going to give it my best shot, dressing up in my favourite gear, my black sneakers, jeans, a long-sleeved white shirt, and red jumper!

I rarely travelled on public transport on my own and my parents would usually accompany me on day trips down to the beach, but this time I chose to go it alone. I drove my car the few minutes it took to get to the Kyneton train station, parking in the disabled parking space, leaving just a short walk from my car to the platform. Boarding the V-Line train from Bendigo, I carefully stepped through the automatic doors and found a seat nearby, placing my sticks by my side, ready for the swiftest exit I could manage at Melbourne's Southern Cross station.

Looking out the window, trying to distract myself from the three million butterflies that were having a dance party in my stomach, I put my headphones on and listened to my favourite tunes, as the rocking of the train caused my involuntary swaying from side to side for what felt much longer than the usual hour-long journey. Finally, as the carriage pulled into the platform at Southern Cross, I carefully navigated my way towards the train's exit, making sure I didn't clumsily lose a stick in the gap or trip and fall flat on my face and embarrass myself.

Safely off the train and standing on the platform, as my eyes desperately waded through an endless sea of strangers, I immediately recognised Yessah's beautiful face, and as she approached me, all I could see was her big, brown eyes and wide smile. She was just as pretty in person as she had been online, and coincidently she also wore a matching red jumper. I was as stuck as if my legs had gone from wobbly jelly to granite. Frozen in my tracks, she continued to make her way over to where I was standing and, gripping my sticks and balancing precariously on my crooked legs, I tried to free up my arms to hug her. At the same time, she stuck out her hand for a handshake which resulted in an awkward hug-shake, which was not at all part of the perfectly co-ordinated, natural embrace I had envisaged in my head. But we both pretended not to notice the weirdness of the moment and, as we walked together to the Melbourne Aquarium, with Yessah patiently slowing her stride so as not to walk ahead of me, my heart melted. I was star-struck.

Trying to project an image of confidence, I held my metal sticks tightly in both hands, putting one in front of the other carefully supporting each step I took, and off we went on our first date.

Yessah was very excited to be visiting the aquarium because, as I would discover, she loved sharks. Unfortunately, unlike the shark that swam around its enclosure with poise and confidence, I felt like a turtle hiding its head within its shell. I was overwhelmed by our meeting and my shyness enveloped me. I couldn't speak. She was kind and beautiful and I was shy and worried about whether she would like me just as I was.

We wandered around the aquarium, observing staff feeding the penguins and divers swimming with the sharks, all of the activity safely taking place behind the thick glass walls separating us from the dangerous would-be ocean dwellers.

Afterwards we stopped for lunch at the aquarium's Croc Café where I chose a chicken wrap. This was the easiest item on the menu for me to hold and eat, without having to juggle cutlery in my trembling fingers. Yessah ordered a burger. I was frozen with nerves and could only manage one syllable answers to Yessah's probing questions. I felt I was failing miserably, I was in total awe just being in the company of a beautiful woman, and felt like I needed a handbook with instructions, like the manual you get when you buy a new television or car. I had no idea what to do next. To be fair, most guys don't bother to read instructions, but this was worse than putting an Ikea bookshelf together. When it was time to go, Yessah insisted we walk back to the train station, instead of catching the tram, as she'd read on my profile that I enjoyed being active and keeping fit. But I may have oversold my level of fitness, because by the time we reached the station, I had sweat dripping down my back and my shirt was wet through—not a very attractive look!

We said goodbye and I gave Yessah a peck on the cheek and sadly we made no further plans to catch up. My journey home on the train was sombre. I pictured Yessah and how beautiful she was and how kind and caring she had been to me, but I had no confidence that I would ever see her again. Just like the other online women, I was afraid my disability had scared her off.

It was starting to get dark as the train pulled into Kyneton. By the time I got home and was safely in the privacy of my bedroom, I realised that I had thought of nothing but Yessah and suddenly found my clumsy hands and fingers reaching for my phone to text her. My thumbs were shaking and it became difficult to text, so I decided I had to call her. I needed to know whether our friendship could continue. I was totally nervous and scared, assuming that her answer would be a flat "no", but I needed to know if my disability was something that she was comfortable with, or if I was wasting my time. Given the caring attitude she showed toward me on our date I shouldn't have been surprised, but Yessah completely shocked me and said that she had enjoyed our date and wanted to see me again. The butterfly dance party kicked off again, but to a much better tune, and inside I was dancing along.

I couldn't believe it! I was ecstatic and felt like one of the single men from reality TV show 'The Bachelorette' who had been handed a red rose and granted another chance to win the heart of the female star who was looking for love.

The early signs were encouraging. We picked up where we left off, FaceTiming every day and then we decided to meet up again the following week, this time in Kyneton at a local pub.

My parents had picked up on my jovial mood and, knowing that I had been in constant contact with a woman, they wanted to meet her. They had always been extra protective of me and done their best to guard me against bullying or being taken advantage of. To put their minds at ease, they needed to know that my friendship with Yessah was something that they could trust and that it would be a positive one for me.

So, I asked them to join us for lunch, but Dad turned down the invitation as he said that he felt too nervous. Yeah right, like he was the nervous one... I had never realised before how similar my Dad and I were, but when it came to nerves, I was definitely my father's son. Mum, however, eagerly accepted the invitation and met us at the pub.

So, there we were, in the middle of the large dining room, the three of us together for lunch and I did it again: my nerves got the better of me and I was cruelly stripped of my ability to speak. I'd never taken a woman out for a meal in my hometown and felt self-conscious, as if everyone was looking at us, instead of tucking into their counter meals. I felt like a canary at a cat show. Everyone eyeing me off, waiting to pounce. The truth was that I felt embarrassed introducing a female friend to my mum, but the two of them hit it off immediately, chatting like they were the best of friends.

They talked about Mauritius and the family Yessah had left behind to travel the world. Mum was probing in a gentle way, wanting to learn more about this new woman who had entered our lives. Later, Mum told me that she couldn't understand why I wasn't more talkative during lunch, but she did agree that Yessah was as beautiful on the inside as she was on the outside and did her best to make her feel welcome.

The following week, Yessah met me in Kyneton again and we ate fish 'n' chips in the Botanic Gardens. I wasn't so shy this time and we were very relaxed with each other while we chatted under the large oak trees that were beginning to lose their autumn leaves. Just as the leaves gently fell after releasing themselves from the almost bare branches, I too felt an inner ease as I slowly began to shed my fear of rejection.

That afternoon, sitting next to each other on the soft grass, we felt a mutual closeness that neither of us had felt before. We loved each other's company and, as my heart began to beat so hard that I thought it would pump out of my chest, I leant in close to her and we expressed our feelings with a kiss. Luckily, we were sitting down because my wobbly legs would almost certainly have failed me had we been standing! It was a precious and unforgettable moment and I felt happier than I'd ever felt before and wished that feeling would last forever.

As the autumn sun began to lose what little warmth it had, I took Yessah back to my house so she could meet my Dad. My parents must have sensed the fact that I was nearly busting out of my skin with elation because when we walked through the door, Mum and Dad couldn't wipe the smiles off their faces. It was actually a little embarrassing and it made me feel like I was a teenager announcing to the world that I finally had a hot date to take to the school dance. Still, it was a special day and, while I had never loved a woman before, I felt after the first couple of dates with Yessah that I was absolutely in love with her. Until this time, I had been terrified that nobody could love me for who I was, but I was starting to feel like this could be the real thing. I felt I'd been dealt a bad hand in life, living with a disability, but finally the stars were aligning for me. Was Yessah falling in love with me, too? The wait for the next rose, was going to take all my patience.

After many weeks of spending treasured moments together and allowing our relationship to blossom, we got to know each other more and more. Everything and everyone looked different to me and I felt as if I'd finally been allowed to enter the exclusive club that usually welcomed anybody else but me. A club where the sky is bluer, the beer is colder, and nothing can bring you down. Like the Collingwood football club.

Then one day out of the blue, Yessah suddenly dropped a bombshell about her past that had crept back into her life. She confided in me that apart from wanting to travel, another reason she had left Mauritius was because she was devastated after ending a two-year relationship with a man she was engaged to. He had been emotionally abusive and controlling, he didn't like the food Yessah cooked and constantly told her she was no good for anything. He had managed to track her down and continued to contact her while she was in Australia, insisting to her that he had changed and wanted to reignite their relationship. Yessah told me that she was torn between making the choice of returning to her ex-partner or continuing our relationship.

I felt absolutely devastated that the beautiful relationship we had built was now at risk of ending. The sadness was overwhelming, and I couldn't imagine losing Yessah, the first woman I had loved and the first woman who I thought was falling in love with me. I also felt deeply saddened and hurt that Yessah had continued to stay in contact with an ex-boyfriend while she was seeing me. Had all of the amazing moments we'd shared as a couple been wasted? I wasn't sure at all if we could overcome this first hurdle and rise above it. This Survivor was not going to leave the island without a fight.

After much soul-searching and many sleepless nights spent pondering the type of future she wanted for herself, thankfully, Yessah chose me. If it was a competition to win over her heart, I had won, and when she told me she could see us having a future together I felt like the luckiest man alive. If I could have done one of those jumps where both of your feet touch while in mid-air, like the new car owners in the Toyota car ads, I would have done that a thousand times. Mum guarded the couch in case my inner Tom Cruise took over. Instead, I dropped my sticks, wrapped my arms around her (I didn't want to fall over) and kissed her.

After that our relationship grew rapidly. We spent every weekend together, and weeknights after work we FaceTimed for hours on end. We wanted to see more of each other, but the distance between our homes meant a four-hour round-trip on public transport just to make this happen. So, in mid-April, just a few months after we'd met, we decided to take a huge step in our relationship. We planned for Yessah to leave Melbourne and come to live in Kyneton with me in our family home. Huge, massive, the biggest move since Plugger went to the Sydney Swans.

Before the move, Yessah secured a job at a local business which, she had made clear, was a prerequisite for her to shift in with us. Yessah resigned from her bakery job in Williamstown and left behind friends and an aunty, also from Mauritius, who lived nearby at Truganina. I couldn't have been happier knowing she was choosing to give life with me a try, trusting that we may have a future together, but I was also very conscious and scared for her because of the sacrifices she was making.

On May twenty third, 2018—my twenty-eighth birthday—Yessah officially moved into my family home and we celebrated her arrival with a roast lamb dinner at the Kyneton RSL where we drank beer and red wine, toasting this new chapter in our lives. We then headed home where Yessah and my parents sang happy birthday to me before we all tucked into a homemade birthday cake.

To cap off a great day, I had phone calls from some of my favourite people that I had developed strong friendships with throughout my life, my football idol, former AFL Collingwood coach Nathan Buckley, and players Jarrod Blair and Jordan DeGoey. I was the happiest I had been ever. It was a perfect day.

So much had happened in our lives over the very short time we had been together, but nobody could have prepared Yessah and I for what was about to happen. Within weeks we would receive news that would change our lives forever.

Chapter Two

Yessah's move into my family home came with many awkward moments, with our sleeping arrangements the first big discussion to be had. We were a young couple just starting out in a very new relationship and were clearly very attracted to one another. But my parents are quite old-fashioned so sleeping together in the same bed under the same roof as them, was a definite no-no! Yessah and I were so incredibly excited at the thought that we would be living in the same town, let alone the same house, so we agreed that she would sleep in the guest room and that I would continue to sleep in my own bedroom. Now, that's not to say we didn't share intimate moments together! We just had to be creative and make the most of the times when we had the house to ourselves. There was also the issue of Yessah's abundance of clothing, and the fact that Mum's wardrobe was equally considerable and spilled over into the spare room. It was decided a cull was necessary and Yessah sorted through her belongings, shedding her least favourite frocks and shoes, donating them to the local op shop.

Yessah's arrival could have also meant an extra cook was now in the house, but I'd have to wait a little longer to be spoilt with her Mauritian curries, dahls and rice dishes she loved to create as Mum and Dad were the 'three meat and veg' types, so those were left off the menu. Assisting with the cooking and cleaning gave Yessah a sense of belonging, but it was the attention to my needs that really made a big difference for my parents.

For the first time in 28 years they were assisted with my daily needs, as Yessah comfortably stepped in to help out. When she wasn't working, Yessah's was the first face I saw most mornings when she came into my room to help get me out of bed. I still couldn't believe how lucky I had been to meet this amazing human; she was the greatest thing that had ever happened to me. Utterly selflessly, Yessah helped me in and out of the shower, helped me put on my underwear and shirt before fitting my splints, then my pants, socks and shoes. I had to pinch myself sometimes, I was so happy. Yessah was more to me than I could have ever imagined. I felt like I'd won the jackpot and my prize was a billion times better than any multimillion-dollar lottery. After all, you can't buy happiness. Just like the roses in our front yard would soon begin to open, our relationship was blossoming, and I was grateful to my parents for welcoming Yessah into our home.

We soon began to venture out more regularly as a couple, firstly around the town and then further afield, discovering the gorgeous Macedon Ranges as if we were tourists, as well as Melbourne's nightlife with its great restaurants and pubs.

It was late one Saturday afternoon when we caught the train from Kyneton to Melbourne where we'd planned for me to meet Yessah's best friend from Mauritius, Kriti, and her husband, Sunil, who were expecting their first child any day. We met at Crown Casino for dinner and I was feeling really nervous and anxious that Yessah's friends would judge me because of my disability.

As I approached them, I could see they were excited to meet me, but I wondered what they were actually thinking. I always wished I could see deeper into people's thoughts and understand how they saw me. I smiled and shuffled towards them as fast as I could, but there was no disguising my cerebral palsy with my uneven strides and my sticks supporting every step I took. However, I need not have worried, as Kriti and Sunil were so very welcoming, and we hugged and shook hands like old friends. At dinner Sunil and I chatted about our work and his new life in Australia, while Yessah and Kriti reminisced about their childhood days in Mauritius. It was fun and relaxed and the four of us had a great night.

Sitting close to one another on the train on our way home, her hand resting in mine, Yessah happily told me that we had Kriti's blessings as a couple. Kriti had said that she could see how much we loved each other, and that we were obviously committed to one another, but she did warn Yessah to be sure that she knew what she was getting into, being in a relationship with me, and the level of commitment she would have to make to not only love me but to care for me, too. I turned and stared through the window, my eyes moving quickly, trying to capture the scenes of the rapidly dancing lights rushing past me. Did Yessah see herself as my lover, or my carer?

The answer to this became clear not long after this outing, one evening when we had the house to ourselves. Out of the blue Yessah dropped the L word and told me she loved me. It had taken her a couple of months since moving into the house to share her most intimate feelings for me, but we'd made it. We set out to give our relationship a go, and Yessah had fallen in love with me. It was a beautiful feeling, and a weight off my shoulders. I was loved by a woman for the first time in my life and it was the most amazing feeling in the world.

Early in June we received the fantastic news that Kriti had given birth to a baby girl named Michaela, and Yessah and I were privileged to be the first visitors to meet her. I didn't really know what to expect about meeting such a tiny, vulnerable person who was so new to this world. During the visit to the maternity ward that smelled of talcum powder and warm, freshly washed towels, I had the honour of being able to hold baby Michaela. Sitting in a chair by the window, my arms propped up with pillows for support, her perfect little body was carefully placed into my arms. As I stared down at her perfect face and her little hand wrapped tightly around my fingers, I was changed forever. It was the most beautiful feeling and from that moment I was overcome with a desperate, unquestionable knowing that one day I wanted to be a father, too.

While Yessah and I had discussed having our own children and realised it was something we both definitely wanted one day, the voices of doctors who had treated me as a young boy still rang loudly in my head. They had told me I probably wouldn't be able to have children of my own, and if I did there would be a chance that they, too, could be born with a disability. These words of warning, however unfounded, stayed with me, haunting me and driving an inner will in me to prove them wrong.

Even in the very early months of our courtship, Yessah and I discussed all avenues of having children—adoption, surrogacy and the sperm donor program—just in case we were unable to conceive naturally by ourselves. After a while it began to weigh heavily on our minds so, instead of dwelling on all of the possibilities, we decided to … well, a gentleman never kisses and tells, but let me just say we decided to have some fun and just see what happened.

Several weeks later, Yessah came into my bedroom early one morning and woke me to say she was getting ready for work. It was her usual routine, but something

If I can, you can

felt different. Noticing a sense of anxiousness about her, I tried to gather as much strength as I could and sat up in bed, a bundle of pillows supporting my back, and asked her what was going on. She explained that she had been feeling unusual lately and didn't quite seem like herself. Then, reaching into her pocket she pulled out a home pregnancy test that she'd done that morning which showed two perfectly straight, short, pink lines. We checked and double-checked the instructions: two lines meant positive, one line meant negative. Yessah was pregnant! The able-bodied Hayden in my head leapt from my bed, grabbed Yessah by the waist and threw her into the air with delight. But the man sitting in my bed calmly asked her if she was sure. With a little, tentative smile, Yessah said she would need it confirmed by the doctor, but she was pretty sure she was pregnant. We gave each other a short but loving kiss and as she left my room to get ready for work, I lay back down in my bed in shock, but with a smile on my face that felt like it could have stretched from one side of my room to the other. Yes! I had proven the doctors wrong! There was no doubt about it, my boys could swim! I felt like I was in the middle of a dream, a wonderful dream.

Ordinarily, waking up in the mornings was a long, slow process due to the heavy medication I was taking for my bipolar disorder that I was diagnosed with in my late teens after my stint in the psych ward. But in those early days, having Yessah as my alarm made getting going in the mornings much easier. Following her shock pregnancy news, I managed to remain awake and called Yessah back into the room after she'd showered and dressed. As she was leaving, I asked her what she would like to call our baby. She simply smiled and waved before blowing me a kiss, and I happily rolled over and dreamily fell back to sleep.

YESSAH

As I walked to work early that morning with the surprise positive pregnancy test in my handbag, I was aware of an array of emotions. I was filled with love for Hayden; I felt apprehension about what lay ahead for us, but also absolute joy at the prospect of becoming a mother. But I was also in shock, so I called my mum in France where it was late at night. As soon as I heard the comforting tone of her voice in our native language, Creole, I began sobbing into the phone, and before I had a chance to tell her, she guessed I was pregnant. I was overwhelmed and desperately wanted her advice. I wished she was by my side so that she could give me a big hug and tell me everything was going to be ok. What she did tell me was to go and see a doctor and get a confirmation of the pregnancy as soon as possible, just to be sure. Deep in my heart there was no question as to whether I would keep the baby or not. I was going to be a mother and Hayden was going to have the baby so many had told him he would never have. I walked the last hundred metres to the bakery where I started work at six AM, *bidding farewell on the phone to my mum, half a world away.*

My adventures Down Under certainly took an unexpected turn when I met Hayden, and dreams of working and travelling came to an abrupt halt.

But I believe it was no accident that Hayden and I were drawn together on an online dating app; we were meant to be together. From the first time I saw his eHarmony profile, I was taken by his good looks, perfect teeth and cheeky smile.

It is true to say I was scared about entering into a relationship with a person living with a disability, and before connecting with Hayden I sought advice from my mother and sister. Trusting their wise words in the past had proven to work out for me, and thankfully I trusted them again as they both told me to follow my heart.

From the first moment I met him, I was absolutely blown away by Hayden's abilities. I was in awe that he could swim, play football, work and drive a car. I thought he was handsome and ambitious, and I could easily see past his cerebral palsy.

I loved watching him achieve his goals and striving to always do his best and I think it was his love of life that really attracted me to him. My past experiences with men had left me with the impression that all men were lazy, but not Hayden. I loved how independent he was, and I loved that he also looked after me. He comforted me when I was sad, he chose the right words to calm me and he always put my feelings before his. Despite being completely different individuals in many ways, we had found each other, and it was amazing.

Before I travelled to Australia, I had worked with children living with disabilities and also had a nephew with autism who lived in France. However, I had never met anyone with cerebral palsy, and I was curious to learn as much as I could about the condition. He astounded me with the full and active life he led, and I thought he was more capable than any boyfriend I had ever had. It seemed like there wasn't anything Hayden couldn't do; he just did things differently.

I came to Australia on a study visa in 2017 when I was 23 years old. I travelled alone with plans to explore other countries and improve my English as Creole, a derivative of French, is my first language. I settled in a relatively new suburb southwest of Melbourne called Williams Landing and enrolled in classes to study English, and later cooking, and dreamed of landing a job on a cruise ship where I could work and travel around the world. I left behind my father and sister in Mauritius, while my mother lived in France with her second husband. I chose Australia because of its warm climate, although I soon discovered Kyneton winters could be very cold and snow had been known to fall in the town. I also considered Australia to be a safe country, at a time when terrorist attacks had been growing more frequent across Europe. Soon after arriving in Melbourne, I picked up work at a bakery and met up with Kriti, my childhood friend from Mauritius. We loved going into the city with friends for drinks after work and going to the beach on sunny days.

I decided to try online dating about a year after arriving in Australia I had made some good friends in Williams Landing but I was keen to find a companion and start dating again.

After meeting Hayden online, then in person, our relationship developed quickly and I became a regular at the Kyneton Football Netball Club where Hayden was a volunteer timekeeper during the senior men's home football games. Hayden also got to know my friends well and we often spoke about our future together.

Being a couple was not hard for the two of us at all, but some people couldn't understand why we had chosen each other. A small number of very close friends shocked me when they assumed that I was using Hayden to get residency in Australia. They said they thought that I would dump him once I became a permanent resident. I was heartbroken by these accusations; how could those close to me even think that I would deliberately use and betray anyone, let alone a man I was growing to love?

When Hayden and I decided that I would move to Kyneton his parents, Brendan and Coral, did their due diligence before welcoming me into their home. They wanted to know what my intentions were and asked what would happen when my study visa expired and how I was going to plan a future with Hayden with this uncertainty. I assured them that we would navigate our way together when the time came to address these issues. I spent many mornings with Brendan, watching how he carefully helped Hayden into the shower, or dried his back afterwards because Hayden couldn't reach far enough to dry himself. He showed me how to gently slip Hayden's feet into his splints, and how to tighten them just enough so they were comfortable and didn't cause Hayden any pain when he walked. He warned me to ensure the floor was dry, so as to avoid Hayden crashing down with his splints on the slippery tiles. When I felt confident enough to take on these tasks myself, Brendan graciously and gratefully handed over the baton. As a result, mine and Hayden's relationship reached another level of closeness neither of us had experienced before.

As I approached my work that morning with the knowledge that I had a tiny, precious life growing inside me, just a few hundred metres from where Hayden was no doubt sleeping soundly, I thought about how on earth Hayden's parents and the rest of our families and friends would react to the news that we were having a baby.

HAYDEN

Later that day Yessah and I visited our local GP, full of hope, angst and trepidation. My life had been filled with visits to doctors and hospitals, but this was different. My complete focus was on Yessah and the tiny baby we suspected was growing within her. After what seemed like an eternity, her doctor delivered the good news, confirming that Yessah was indeed pregnant.

As we made our way towards the door to leave, I couldn't get over the thought of how lucky we had been to conceive a baby so easily. After all those years of being told I wouldn't become a father, here we were, just four months into our relationship pregnant with our very own creation. While other patients sat stony faced in the doctors' waiting room, eyes glued to their mobile phones, Yessah and I may as well have been in another world, with smiles from ear to ear. But a stark reality soon began to sink in: now we had to reveal our news to Mum and Dad.

Sitting next to each other at the dinner table that night, Yessah and I looked at my unsuspecting parents and, with our sweaty hands holding on tightly to each other, told them we had some news. Casually taking another mouthful of her beef stew, an absolute favourite in our house, Mum mumbled, 'Yeah?' Seeing as it would have taken me another 20 minutes to get the words out of my slow-moving mouth, Yessah nervously told them we were expecting a baby.

Nearly choking on her stew, Mum threw a shocked look at Dad, then at us, then at Dad again and neither of them could speak. Eventually, as if they'd both finally processed that Yessah was actually speaking in English and suddenly understood what she was saying, they asked if the pregnancy had been confirmed. Trying to hide their concern and hesitation, they anxiously asked when scans could be taken of the baby because, just as we both had fears ourselves, my parents also worried. We all wanted evidence that the latest addition to our family would be healthy. As if suddenly remembering that this type of announcement was usually met with congratulatory cries and screams of joy, Mum and Dad could see how happy we were with our news and with a warm, nurturing embrace, Mum gave us each a big, tight hug. We all finished our dinner feeling excited and nervous for what lay ahead.

Yessah's parents were also shocked, and naturally scared for their daughter who already had a disabled partner. Naturally we all wanted a healthy baby, but we knew from the first moment the pregnancy was confirmed, that we would love our baby unconditionally, no matter what. Everybody was praying for us before we attended the first ultrasound.

Around the same time that we found out about the baby, we had decided that living with my parents wasn't going to cut it for much longer. As a couple we needed our privacy and our own space, and now with news of the baby, we were even more sure we needed to move out and set up a home of our own. The only downside to this was having to leave my dog Bella with Mum and Dad, as most real estate agents wouldn't allow pets in their rentals. I would miss her, and I was upset, but Dad promised we could go for walks with her as often as we liked. During past walks, Dad held Bella's lead while I rode my red three-wheeler tricycle, a means of transport that served me well for well over two decades. I immediately had visions of future walks/rides that would include Yessah, a pram and our baby joining in this special family ritual.

Rental offerings in Kyneton were pretty slim and the first house we looked at was snapped up by another couple before we even had a chance to put in an application. Luckily for us though, a local real estate agent was a friend of my aunty and we were soon told about a small, 2-bedroom unit that was empty, available for rent and perfect for us. It was the second in a set of four units built behind an older, period-style home that had a road frontage position. The entrance to our unit was at ground level, which meant there wouldn't be any access problems for me, or a pram! The landlords accepted our application and we signed the contract immediately.

So, as the biting winter fell upon Kyneton, we moved into our new home. Outside it was icy cold, but inside we couldn't have been warmer or happier, together, expecting our first baby.

As a couple we grew up very quickly. Throughout the entire pregnancy, I drove Yessah to all of her doctor's appointments and scans. Our first ultrasound was booked at Kyneton Hospital to determine when we could expect to meet our amazing new little bundle.

When I saw the small bean-shaped image on the screen with its beating heart, my own heart leapt in my chest with joy and apprehension. According to the sonographer, the baby was due to arrive in March 2019.

Straining my brain to remember which one of our 'creative moments' had been the successful one, I was able to calculate that conception must have been the night that the Kyneton Tigers' senior men's footy team defeated Kangaroo Flat by 121 points at the Kyneton Showgrounds. I must have been feeling pretty happy after that game!

Imagining our future child playing footy one day, I proudly exclaimed to Yessah, "We're going to have our own little Tiger!"

While our overriding emotions were those of joy and happiness, like most couples about to embark on parenthood for the first time, it was also impossible not to be at least a little bit worried and anxious about what the future held for us. Whilst we were reasonably comfortable in the knowledge that cerebral palsy was not a genetic condition and was not passed on from parents to their children, this did not allay the fears of our closest relatives. There were those who worried for Yessah that if our baby was disabled, she would spend the rest of her life caring for both a partner and a child with disabilities.

Finding out we were pregnant was a huge surprise, but once we embraced it, we never looked back. We were so grateful that it happened so quickly for us. In fact, just one month after we visited Kriti in hospital with her newborn, Michaela, we were pregnant too!

During our baby's eight-week scan we nervously sat in the waiting room knowing that the ultrasound results would determine the path ahead for us as parents. Would our baby enter the world perfectly with the certainty that all parents dreamt of and prayed for? Or would we be confronted with unexpected news, just as my parents had been almost three decades earlier?

YESSAH

It was July 2018, and I was 24 when I found out I was pregnant. My family will attest to the fact that I have wanted nothing more than to one day become a mother, so falling pregnant was a celebration for both Hayden and me, particularly as he had been told he may not be able to ever father a child.

Our unborn baby was our lucky charm. My parents' marriage did not work out, and my mother moved away from our family in Mauritius and lived in Ireland. Like mother, like daughter, Mum met her new partner online and went to live with him in France, leaving me to raise my younger sister in Mauritius, and so my maternal instincts kicked in early as a young girl.

Hayden was unlike any other man I had ever met. He was caring and considerate and always put my needs first.

When we decided to move into our own unit, Hayden suggested that we get a carer funded through his National Disability Insurance Scheme plan to help out with his daily needs. I told him I loved him and wanted to continue helping him by carrying out the morning routine I had begun at his parents' home. But before long, the tables had turned and Hayden became my carer and provider, particularly when I was very unwell with morning sickness. The sheer smell of meat was enough to make me vomit, so I stuck to simply eating toast, eggs, cheese, yoghurt, fruit and fish. On the odd occasion when I cooked meat for Hayden's dinner, I paid the price afterwards becoming violently ill.

My job ended soon after I told the owners I was pregnant, which was disappointing, as it was the first time I had been unemployed since entering the workforce and it didn't sit well with me. I had no income and was unable to receive welfare benefits while on a study visa. But Hayden happily supported me with income from his two jobs at Woolworths and Vicroads and his disability allowance, paying all of our bills, including my study fees and medical bills. While studying full time I was able to get student health insurance, but I soon found that I had to give up my beloved cooking and English classes as the cost and time required were too demanding. Unfortunately, this put an end to my health cover, so I was very grateful to Hayden for supporting me.

During this incredibly stressful time, I started to wonder if having the baby was the right thing to do. But as he so often did, Hayden put my mind at ease, reassuring me that our lucky charm was the most important part of our world and that all would be ok.

I had long distance conversations with my mother in France, questioning whether I should go back to Mauritius to deliver the baby and then return to Australia, as I would have been covered by my native government's health system. Health cover was soon becoming our biggest concern so we were relieved when we discovered that if I was successful in my application for a temporary partner visa, I would be eligible for Medicare cover in Australia. Hayden's parents could see the stress we were experiencing and agreed to pay the $7,000 for my temporary partner visa application, which was thankfully approved. We were both very grateful, and this gave us comfort knowing we could birth our baby in a public hospital in Australia with very few extra costs involved.

I couldn't believe how lucky I was to have Hayden and his parents who loved and supported me unconditionally throughout these difficult and uncertain times.

And the support from Brendan and Coral didn't end there. It was Boxing Day, 2018 and I was six months pregnant when we all decided to go to the Boxing Day sales to do some shopping for the baby. We had put as much money aside as possible, including cash that Hayden's parents had given us for Christmas, to help with setting up the nursery. I had also picked up a job at an aged-care facility in a nearby town where I was employed as a food services assistant. Thankfully the morning sickness had subsided by then! The small amount I earned also went toward our baby's needs, things like a cot, pram, change table, nappies, clothes and toys.

We had reached the end of our shopping spree, where we'd spent every cent we had, when I suddenly realised that we didn't have any baby bottles! We were both excited at the thought of being able to share all of the feeds between us so I couldn't believe this important item wasn't on our list. Without even a blink of his eye, Brendan paid the extra $125 for the bottles and accessories and we left the shops with a feeling of hope, happiness and thankfulness. Brendan and Coral are wonderful people who have treated me just like their own daughter, for which I will be forever grateful.

As the pregnancy progressed more people in the town became aware of our exciting news and congratulated Hayden and me on our impending parenthood. But I was shocked and disappointed by some people who had misunderstood our relationship. We would regularly do the grocery shopping together at Woolworths where Hayden worked and on one occasion, when Hayden did the shopping on his own, a colleague asked him, "Your carer didn't come shopping with you today?" This assumption that I was Hayden's carer deeply concerned me. Was this the way people really saw me? Why couldn't they accept that I was his partner, his lover? What was so unusual about that? People with disabilities had relationships, too! I wondered just how widespread this way of thinking was throughout the town. Did they really believe that I'd just waltzed into town to care for Hayden and got pregnant? I found these stories very upsetting, but Hayden assured me that the people who really mattered—his family and friends—loved me and understood that what we had was real. And I knew he was right; I was very proud of Hayden and our relationship, and very excited about becoming a mother for the first time.

Thankfully, most people were wonderful and accepted me with open arms. I enjoyed so much about country living, especially going to the local French-inspired café and patisserie, Monsieur Pierre, where I bought cheeses and delicacies that reminded me of Mauritius. Back home there was a very strong French influence on every part of our lives, so it was nice to be able to have a sweet or savoury reminder of that any time I wanted. And believe me, those times became more and more frequent as I gave in to my pregnant body's cravings! At the local footy club Hayden's mates and their partners were also very friendly, accepting me and our relationship. They all treated him as one of the boys, as one of their mates, which I discovered was very much the Australian way.

His parents remained very protective of Hayden and kept close tabs on him in those early months of our relationship, as well as during the pregnancy. On New Year's Eve in 2018, Hayden and I were invited to my cousin's home in Ballarat for a party. Hayden drove us the 90 kilometres there, texting his mother when we arrived to let her know we were there safely. I was nervous for Hayden, too, as it was the first time that he had met any of my relatives, who all spoke Creole.

Luckily, they also spoke English and Hayden was naturally welcomed into the group and everyone loved him and accepted him immediately. He was kept well hydrated with beers, not having to move from his stool where he held court with my cousins who were eager to learn more about him. The party was a lot of fun, and we stayed the night at my cousin's house, sparing Hayden another journey home in the dark. I did my best to keep my eyes open until midnight when we shared a tender kiss with excited thoughts about the new year ahead. Our baby was due in March and we were eagerly anticipating what that would mean for our new little family.

Chapter Three

I was going to be a father! I still had to pinch myself to believe that I could be holding my own child in a matter of months. As Yessah's stomach swelled, so too did my sense of pride and excitement at our impending parenthood. I spent a lot of time remembering my own childhood and reflecting on how life would have been for my parents after I came into their world.

*

I was born on the 23rd of May 1990 at the Mercy Maternity Hospital in East Melbourne. Even before I was born, it was evident that I wasn't going to make life easy for Mum. Her pregnancy had been complicated as she had suffered maternal hypertension and pre-eclampsia, dangerous conditions for both her and for me. It was a shaky start, with her being rushed to hospital by ambulance at 35 weeks into the pregnancy. Technically, I still had another 5 weeks left to grow before my due date on July 1st, but that wasn't to be. I was delivered by emergency caesarean at 12:36 in the afternoon and immediately after my birth I suffered respiratory distress and was resuscitated with a low concentration of oxygen, the doctors using a mask and bag.

The *Apgar Score* is a common test given to newborns within their first minutes of life to determine how well they are coping. Doctors considered my heart rate, breathing, muscle tone, skin colour and reflexes before assessing how my entrance into the world would be rated. My score, at one minute, was six out of 10, which generally indicates a baby's health is only fair. However, with the second test carried out at five minutes, I scored a reassuring eight out of 10.

There was no major cause for alarm, everybody considered me to be a perfectly healthy baby boy and I was placed in a humidicrib for a few days to stabilise my temperature as I had a mild case of jaundice, a condition that turns baby's skin yellow and is common in premature babies.

Despite my sudden, dramatic and early arrival, my birth was an exciting time for my parents. Mum and I stayed in hospital for a total of 25 days, giving her plenty of time to begin her recovery from surgery. Nowadays, a 25-day stay in hospital is unheard of. Some mothers and their infants are out the door on the same day if the birth is uncomplicated. Even after having caesarean sections, some women and their babies are discharged within just a few days.

After three and a half weeks, Mum and Dad took me home to start our new life together in Kyneton. They had only been married for three months and Dad was 41, Mum was 40. It was Mum's second marriage and Dad's first; Mum had two sons from her first marriage, who lived with their father. I would be their one and only child together.

I was a happy and bubbly baby. I fed well and I was reaching my growth milestones just as every healthy baby should.

Mum (not being at all biased, of course!) considered me to be a particularly photogenic newborn and believed I had a good chance of winning baby shows with my adorable smile. She entered me into competitions at shopping centres near Melbourne and, sure enough, she was right; I won loads of first prizes. Luckily for me, my looks would hold me in good stead for my online pursuit of love almost 30 years later!

However, despite feeding and growing well, and outwardly appearing happy and content, tell-tale signs began to emerge that I wasn't developing like other babies my age. As my first birthday approached my parents and grandmother were concerned that I was unable to roll, and I wasn't crawling or pulling myself up to stand.

Two days after I turned one, Mum took me to see our local family GP, Dr Andrew Shipley, who examined me before sending Mum away with a referral to the Royal Children's Hospital (RCH).

The RCH is considered the leading paediatric hospital in Australia and recognised world-wide for its high levels of care for sick children, technological advancements and research. The hospital referral read:

"Dear Doctor, I would appreciate if this child could be seen in your Outpatients Department. He is now twelve months old and is not sitting properly. Physically he seems to be okay with no abnormal neurological signs, but this would appear to be quite a significant delay on his milestone development."

I can only imagine how my parents must have felt, not knowing why I couldn't sit up, crawl or stand like other babies Mum had observed in her mothers' group. Did my parents think the worst? Or were they hoping I was just a lazy baby, taking my time to reach milestones that children younger than me were already achieving?

Our appointment at the Children's Hospital was with paediatrician Anton Harding, who examined me in his rooms in the old, yellow, clinker brick building on Flemington Road in Parkville, not far from the centre of Melbourne.

Dr Harding's report in response to Dr Shipley arrived on 25th June, 1991, when I was 13 months old, and would mark the beginning of our new world. The letter began well:

"On examination, Hayden was a happy, chubby baby, who responded well socially. The upper and lower limbs had increased tone (which suggested stiffness) but good range of movement. The rest of the neurological examination was normal, and his head circumference was on the 50th percentile as it had been previously."

All was sounding fine and Dr Shipley would have been encouraged by the letter's positive tone. However, the very next paragraph made a brief reference to my mother's sister, whom I knew had died when she was a baby but mysteriously, I never knew why.

"As you know the family history, I will not go into it further, apart from an aunt that was known to be crippled from the waist down and died at 4 months of age."

Then these prophetic words from Dr Harding:

"Andrew, I wondered whether Hayden has mild cerebral palsy and so have organised a creatine kinase test and brain CT scan. In the meantime, I have suggested to his mother that physiotherapy is required to help mobilise his limbs."

The reason for the creatine kinase (CK) test, a blood test, was to check if the CK enzyme had leaked through my muscle membranes which would indicate muscle damage. And it was hoped that a brain scan might further explain my delayed physical development.

While the word *disability* didn't appear to be used in any of my early medical documentation, the reference to cerebral palsy was undoubtably the diagnosis that handed me an unrequested ticket into the disability world. Interestingly enough, even to this day my parents still don't talk about my diagnosis. Having to consider the words 'cerebral palsy' in reference to their one-year-old baby boy must have been such an emotionally difficult time for them. Now, they simply refuse to relive that period by speaking about it.

My requests for them to contribute to this book were politely refused, and I respect their decision to remain silent about the pregnancy and my birth, as well as their desire to "look to the future and not to the past". As a result, I have relied heavily on my medical records from the Mercy Hospital where I was born, and the Royal Children's Hospital where I received treatment, to tell my story. These medical records document every hospital visit, procedure and medication I have ever received at both facilities.

Reading through my records and reliving the dozens of operations and procedures I have endured throughout my life has been confronting, yet it's part of my journey and one I am proud to share. And it's not an uncommon journey for the thousands of children who receive a CP diagnosis in Australia and around the world every year.

My CT scan was scheduled as a day procedure at the Royal Children's Hospital on the 9th of August. I was almost 15 months old and my developmental delay continued to be worrying for my parents. I was sedated during the procedure so that my wriggling wouldn't hinder the precise cross-section images the radiologists needed to capture of my brain.

It was two long months for my parents before they were requested to attend Dr Harding's rooms at the RCH for the results of the scan. These showed signs of some brain tissue damage, a condition called periventricular leukomalacia, or PVL, sometimes associated with prematurity. Dr Harding was not convinced this was the cause of my developmental delays, though. In his letter to my doctor, he wrote:

"*This condition is secondary to a brain insult, possibly in early pregnancy. It can be associated with prematurity, but I believe Hayden's course (birth) was fairly straightforward following an emergency delivery at 35 weeks' gestation.*"

The reports suggested that my disability was triggered when I suffered a brain injury in the early stages of Mum's pregnancy. Exactly how this happened, I doubt I will ever know. It's highly likely that neither Mum nor Dad ever knew, either.

Having access to the medical records has given me a deep insight into Mum's pregnancy and my birth, and it is comforting for me to learn more about these circumstances and why I was born with a disability, even if the actual cause remains a mystery.

The final paragraph of Dr Harding's letter about me, then nearly 17 months old, read:

"*His ultimate prognosis is difficult to give, apart from the fact that his development should continue, but slowly.*" The next appointment was planned for three months' time.

In a follow-up letter to Dr Shipley, Dr Harding said, "*I have suggested to the parents that Hayden's motor development will be very slow but that I was pleased to hear he was now starting to roll in both directions.*"

By December the same year I was 19 months old and it was widely accepted that I had cerebral palsy. While my CP was diagnosed as mild, I would need ongoing physiotherapy to treat tight muscles in my legs that hindered my mobility, as well as many other health issues. I had my first physiotherapy assessment at the Anne

Caudle Centre in Bendigo, a regional city larger than Kyneton but smaller than Melbourne. A branch of the Bendigo health system, it was the site of the original Bendigo Benevolent Asylum and its original purpose in 1961 was to "*relieve the aged and infirm, the disabled and the destitute of all creeds and nations*". Essentially, it was a residence for those discarded by society, a place where neglected and disabled children were sent to live from as early as the 1860's. I consider myself a bit of a 'glass half full' kind of guy, so while there are plenty of reasons I could bitch and moan about being born with a disability, one thing I am grateful for is the era into which I was born.

Malcolm Gladwell wrote in his best-selling novel 'Outliers', that "*The sense of possibility so necessary for success comes not just from inside us or from our parents. It comes from our time: from the particular opportunities that our place in history presents us with.*" Fortunately for me, by the early 90's when I was just a young child, the Victorian Government was transforming its public mental health system, introducing deinstitutionalisation. People with intellectual and physical disabilities were removed from psychiatric residential institutions and placed back into the communities of their birth. I see myself as one of the lucky ones, born at a time with parents who never turned their back on me. They gave me every chance in the world to succeed, and I owe all of my successes to them.

I was just a toddler during one of my visits to the Anne Caudle Centre where it was observed that my main means of movement was by rolling, and I had started to pull myself forward on the mat. Mum had told the paediatric physiotherapist that I could also pull myself up to a kneeling position in my cot. My lower legs remained very tight and I began receiving exercises to stretch out my muscles so that eventually I would be able to stand with support.

Before leaving this consultation, my mum was told that I would also benefit from an overall program to stimulate my speech and fine motor skills and was given a referral to the Golden North Centre in Bendigo, a branch of the Spastic Society of Victoria.

The dictionary defines the word 'spastic' as "people born with a disability who are unable to control their muscles, particularly their arms and legs". Unfortunately, this word has also morphed into an offensive, general description of people with disabilities, and more commonly, a slang word to describe able-bodied people who appear uncoordinated. However, I can honestly say, I have never been called a spastic to my face.

I attended the Golden North Centre on several occasions from 1992 and was later happy to hear that in 2001 the Spastic Society of Victoria changed its name to Scope. This move was made to reflect the growth in the organisation, but also to truly reflect their core belief which is to support every person with a disability who has 'scope' to achieve their goals in life.

Australians living with disability make up around 20 per cent of the population and even the language around disability is changing. People With Disability Australia (PWDA) is a national disability advocacy organisation that has established guidelines for the Australian media. PWDA recommends that people with disability are no longer 'wheelchair bound' but referred to as wheelchair users. They recommend the identity of the person always comes first, i.e., a paraplegic becomes a person with paraplegia, and that words like 'able-bodied' or 'healthy' person should be interchanged with 'non-disabled person' or 'person without disability'. These subtle yet powerful changes to our language are baby steps toward society accepting that people living with disabilities should be treated with respect. We want to be treated as equal to others, and we want to control when, how, and *if* we are to be treated differently. For example, I don't expect to be asked if I need help to get out of my car; if I need help, I will ask for it. I understand people want to be kind and offer assistance, but I want them to realise that I have the ability to do most things. I will do them by myself, just usually slower than most, and a little differently.

When I was a toddler, my parents were told by a trusted health professional that because of my cerebral palsy I would never be able to walk unassisted. This was a devastating forecast for Mum and Dad, a prediction that I would be a wheelchair user for the rest of my life. Fortunately, my parents refused to accept this prognosis. They didn't settle for just one professional opinion and their journey began to get me walking independently.

During physiotherapy sessions I had slowly progressed from moving around on my tummy to 'bum shuffling', to crawling. Eventually, I managed to kneel, then pull myself up to a standing position, hanging onto a couch or chair. Not long before my second birthday I was fitted with my AFO's. This extra support provided stability for me when I got to a standing position. But when my physiotherapist tried to help me walk, I tended to cross my legs over. This was attributed to my poor ability to weight transfer while standing.

As well as my mobility issues, I had other health problems which required ongoing attention by more specialists at the RCH. We were lucky enough to live just a one-hour drive from the hospital, where some of the best health experts in their fields practiced. The RCH became my home away from home, and to this day I still reap the benefits of the many surgeries and treatments I endured at the hospital. Anton Harding was involved with my early diagnosis, as well as my ongoing care for over a decade, often referring me to see other specialists. He asked the resident ophthalmologist to see me when I was two-and-a-half to assess a squint in my left eye. It was decided that I would undergo a type of therapy to fix the squint which included wearing a pirate-style patch for a few hours a day. Mum laughs when she tells me that, in order to get me to wear the eye patch, she had to convince me that I could pretend to be Captain Feathersword from The Wiggles and I would spend the whole time saying, "Ahoy there, me hearties!" and she would have to reply with, 'Ahoy there, Captain Feathersword!"

But the patch was only a temporary fix and I would be required to have surgery for a more permanent solution later the following year. That surgery resulted in me developing another squint and having to undergo the same operation again. Unfortunately, the second surgery was not successful either. It was disappointing for me to learn years later that further research had determined my eye problem would most likely have corrected itself without any surgical intervention. As it turned out, thankfully it did just that and within a few years, my squint disappeared.

My paediatrician kept my local doctor in the loop with regular reports about my progress following each visit. When I was three and a half, Dr Harding advised Dr Shipley: "*Andrew, Hayden continues to progress well physically and was able to demonstrate that he could crawl, sit with his legs out in front of him and walk around furniture with some confidence. I believe he also now has a bicycle with training wheels which he rides forwards and backwards!*"

Reading this medical report put a smile on my face because, while I couldn't walk by myself, that wasn't stopping me from getting around on my bike like all the other kids my age. My desire from very early on was to achieve the things other children were achieving; my strong sense of determination is a characteristic I have never lost. Striving to be the best I can be is something I have pursued for as long as I can remember, and I still continue to do. I don't see my disability as a hinderance to my abilities, but rather as an integral part of my unique life journey. For all of the hurdles I have to face, I know there are many more people who face worse obstacles than I. I committed a long time ago to making the most of what I can do, not focusing on what I can't do. Having a disability doesn't stop me from dreaming the same dreams as people without disabilities. Having a fulfilling life is absolutely achievable for people living with disabilities; we want good general health, happy families and to contribute to the workforce, just like most people. My journey has been full of opportunities, disappointments, successes and failures, just like yours and I suspect that I'm just as excited about my future, as you are about yours.

By the age of four I was referred to the RCH Department of Child Development and Rehabilitation where a range of specialists dealt with my various health needs. I had an occupational therapist, a speech pathologist and a social worker.

A summary of my progress in the May of 1994 reported, "*Hayden walks with the assistance of a Kaye Walker.*" This was a metal frame with three sides that sat around me and was open at the front. It had four wheels—two in front of me and two behind—and I held onto the frame that came up to my waist. The report continued, "*He is able to sidestep. He can pull to stand and hang on.*

With regard to the upper limbs, he spoon-feeds himself, but messily! He drinks from a cup. Toilet training has been achieved. His mother does not have any concerns about his communication skills and reports that he talks well."

Not much has changed with respect to my messy eating! I often still drop food or spill drinks on my clothes because of my sometimes shaky or trembling hands, and after a couple of beers it's even worse! My speech has improved thanks to years of speech pathology and I no longer stutter, but my speech can sound slow and slurred, particularly when I am tired.

Before I started school, my parents and physiotherapists came up with a clever idea to ensure I was getting enough walking time with my Kaye Walker, and not relying too much on my wheelchair. A lack of activity is one of the major concerns for people living with CP, which can result in worsening muscle tightness and weight gain. Even today, if I slack off with my physio exercises, my muscles gradually stiffen up and on a cold day I can end up feeling like I have the body of a ninety-year-old man. So, my walker was strapped to the back of my wheelchair, allowing for easy access and a swift transition from sitting to walking if I'd been sedentary for too long.

As my parents and treating physicians prepared me for the next big step in my life, primary school, uppermost in my parents' minds was whether they would ever be able to help me achieve my biggest hurdle yet, to walk independently, without the aid of my walker.

Chapter Four

I was four-and-a-half when I started kindergarten at the Lady Brooks Centre in Kyneton. Mum or Dad would push me to kinder in my wheelchair and then I'd be moved from a seated position to my Kaye Walker to help me get around the classrooms. My most vivid memories stem from playing outside on the historic milk wagon that took pride of place in the centre's front yard, and still does today. Getting into the wagon was a challenge, but my teachers happily hitched me up high enough for me to grab hold of the steering wheel and pull myself into the driver's seat. My integration aide, Lisa Boyer, remembers me being like 'a bull at a gate' in my walker. She feared I'd end up flat on my face and I often had to be slowed down. The thing was that I just wanted to get to the activities and lunch tables as quickly as I could. I never wanted to be left behind. I had a go at everything and refused to let my disability exclude me from group activities. I clumsily fed myself cut-up pieces of fruit and drank from a cup like all the other children at morning tea. I played in the sandpit and also loved painting where I would stand, supported by my walker in front of the easel where I finger painted pictures of the sky and the sea. As I could only reach halfway up the page, my teachers would flip my painting around when I filled the bottom half so that I could continue filling the rest of the page with more paint. Despite my crooked fingers, these finger paintings were some of my finest artworks! I also sat on the floor and created buildings with coloured blocks, I sang songs and played musical instruments and took a particular liking to the guitar; my fingers managed strumming the vinyl strings quite well. The teachers say I never felt sorry for myself because of my cerebral palsy, I never gave up and the other kinder kids accepted me exactly as I was. I think I developed a thick skin very early and just got on with the task at hand to the best of my ability.

I do remember feeling a little sad at times though, when I was sitting by myself, unable to keep up with the other kids who ran out of the classroom and into the yard. But I learnt to deal with these feelings and just got on with it. I made friends and had play dates with other children while our mums drank cups of tea and ate cake. The other four- and five-year-olds were not judgemental at all. It was as if they didn't even notice my disability; to them I was just another kid and that's exactly what I wanted to be. Towards the end of my kindergarten year my mobility was deteriorating because of the tightness in my legs, despite my regular physiotherapy. It was around this time that I was referred to orthopaedic surgeon Professor Graham Kerr, at the RCH. Professor Kerr had been leading his field with research into improving outcomes for children with CP, particularly the use of botulinum toxin injections, commonly known as Botox. In a letter to my paediatrician at the end of 1995, Professor Kerr wrote, "At the age of 5 and a half years, Hayden walks quite well with a 'Kaye' postural walker, but he has quite considerable difficulties because of dynamic contractures of his hamstrings, adductors and calf muscles. I think that it would be very reasonable to consider intervention with botulinum toxin injections. There will be a study into the benefits of these injections within the hospital next year, and I think that Hayden would be eligible for inclusion."

I would have to wait several months before my inclusion in the trial began, but that didn't bother me because I had exciting times ahead with the impending summer holidays before I was to begin my first year at primary school.

I spent most summer holidays in the Melbourne bayside suburb of Brighton. My Dad's brother, Tom, his wife, Marcia, and their five children welcomed me into their home as one of their own. They lived in a two-storey house with lots of bedrooms upstairs, and because of my regular visits they refurbished the downstairs part of the house to ensure I had easy access to everywhere I needed. These vacations gave me an opportunity to explore the beach and spend time with my cousins, while Mum and Dad had a well-deserved break from caring for me.

But my adventurous tendencies sometimes got me into strife during these wonderful holidays. On one occasion Uncle Tom, who was also my godfather, agreed to take me out kayaking. However, my enthusiasm in the kayak backfired in the ocean near the Brighton Yacht Club when we both came dangerously close to being tipped out of the vessel. We were both perched on our own end of the kayak, me with my precarious grip around the oars doing my best to contribute, but then I got distracted and began daydreaming and stopped rowing, and the boat began tilting heavily to the side Uncle Tom was on. He was angry with me as he had trusted that I would pull my weight, and he swore he would never take me out kayaking again!

He did, however, think it was safe enough to take me to AFL games to see my Collingwood Magpies play his beloved North Melbourne Kangaroos, and these became annual outings together which I looked forward to every year, even when the Kangaroos beat the Magpies! My summer family became a constant in my life, and I longed for the holidays as this was where I developed my love of the beach and the ocean. It was often hard work making my way through the sand using my Kaye Walker, and on occasions when I got bogged, I resorted to crawling just to keep up with the gang.

My mischievous ways also got me into strife back at the house once when I secretly shared my stash of lollies Mum had packed for me with my two younger cousins, Madelaine and Monique. Auntie Marcia, who was strict like my Dad, gave me a good piece of her mind, reminding me that the girls, who were just a couple of years younger than me, were not allowed to eat lollies. They were, however, allowed to make their own lemonade, which was full of sugar! We used to set up stalls at the front of their house and sell it for one dollar a cup to anyone who walked by.

I was included as a family member and treated no differently to the rest of my cousins and I absolutely loved it.

After graduating from kinder it was time for me to start my formal education and my parents chose a small, independent primary school in Tylden, about 16 kilometres west of Kyneton. Thankfully for me, Principal Rob Taylor was ahead of his time and had been integrating children with disabilities into the mainstream school system for over a decade. As a result, the school had a very good reputation for providing programs that helped children with disabilities to learn and be the best they could be, which, fittingly, was also the school's motto: 'Be your best'.

The December before I started at Tylden Primary I was assessed by an occupational therapist and physiotherapist with the report then being sent to Principal Taylor outlining my disabilities. This also came with a recommendation that I be provided with a full-time integration aide for every day I attended school. The report said I was a five-and-a-half-year-old boy who relied upon a walking frame for mobility. I was only able to walk short distances with the Kaye Walker and required supervision to ensure my safety. I needed help moving from positions like standing and sitting and often had falls when attempting to sit down. The report noted that in the playground, "Hayden has difficulty negotiating uneven surfaces and other obstacles, i.e., children."

Due to the slight squint in my eyes, I had poor balance and visual difficulties. I also had problems holding and manipulating objects as my fine motor skills were hindered due to muscle tightness in my fingers. My movements were slow and awkward, which meant I required more time to finish tasks. The report went on to say, "Hayden's speech is slow and difficult to understand. He has difficulty with coordinating the movements of his face, tongue, mouth and lips. He needs reminders to keep to task as his concentration is poor and he is easily distracted."

Reading these reports has had a profound impact on me. I did not recognise my five-year-old self at all. There was no mention of the happy, independent and positive person I am today, and probably was then too. I remember having a fun time, digging in the sandpit, kicking the footy on the oval and playing with my friends. I understand the report had a distinct purpose, which was to support the need for an integration aide during the hours I was at school, but I wish it could have also included a summary of my positive personality, my uplifting spirit, my cheeky smile and my many abilities.

Tylden Primary School was set in a small rural community and backed onto the local sports oval. Every year the school hosted the Tylden Fair with events such as the vintage tractor pull, which was an annual highlight for locals and those from surrounding towns, and a great fundraiser for the school. I loved that my mum and grandma baked cakes and volunteered on the stalls. Within the school grounds a vegetable garden and chook house formed part of the daily curriculum with students being responsible for feeding the chooks, collecting the eggs and tending to the veggie patch. My mum didn't like me coming home with dirty knees or a dirty school uniform, so, unbeknownst to her, the teachers put plastic down on the ground so that I could potter around in the garden and the dirt, while staying reasonably clean. On days when I still managed to get really dirty (after all, I was still a grubby little kid!), they would strip me down, dress me in clothes from the lost property collection, wash my clothes and redress me in my clean school uniform before Mum picked me up at 3:30pm. I always felt a bit cheeky and naughty doing that, but I was so grateful to those caring teachers who recognised how invaluable my 'getting down and dirty' was for my emotional development.

Like kindergarten, at primary school I was supported by my Kaye Walker and had my wheelchair as backup. There were ramps that gave me easy access to classrooms, and concrete paths meandered around the schoolyard leading to play areas, entrances and exits. In the classroom, teachers planned a three-month program of schoolwork with specific goals that were achievable for me to reach, like counting or learning new words. I worked hard and got a real kick out of learning to read and write, but my favourite part of school was playing with the other kids at playtimes, or when we went outside for sport.

Mrs Janet Cole was my grade four teacher, and she was also the school's softball and T-ball coach. When it was time for me to bat during our weekly sports lessons, she would place the ball on a stand, help me grip the bat and then stand back so I could take a big swing and hit the ball as far as I could. I had a runner who sprinted to each base for me as I continued to hit the ball until I was caught out or my runner was run out. My classmates were mostly supportive and encouraged me to go hard when playing sport, even though I didn't have the speed and strength that they had. They cheered me on and were happy to have me on their teams. I was encouraged to get involved and treated like one of the boys.

However, there were the occasional bullies who didn't like the attention I was getting, or felt that I ruined their games and tried to exclude me. At these times I felt sad and would sit by myself, or my integration aide would take me to the cubby house and help me climb into it, giving me a hoist up the ladder.

As I grew taller during my prep year, the tightness in my leg muscles increased, making it painful to run or even walk with my walker. Professor Kerr decided it was time to be included in the RCH study to determine whether Botox injections would give me any pain relief and improve my mobility. On the day the Botox trial began, all I can remember is squealing in pain as the doctors started hacking into my calves and hamstrings with giant needles. At least, that's what it felt like; it hurt like Hell! Imagine getting this in your face and paying for it!

After a few minutes, when my legs were numb and my eyes finally stopped running like a tap, Professor Kerr injected a total of 96 small doses of Botox into my upper and lower legs, paralysing some muscles and blocking the nerves that had been causing me so much pain. It took a few days for the Botox to take effect, but when it did, what a relief! The pain and stiffness subsided, enabling me to move much more freely. These injections, in conjunction with physiotherapy, helped for about six months, but for me that wasn't nearly long enough. I had to wait another six months before I was eligible for another round of injections, but it was becoming clear that the tightness in my hamstrings was causing an abnormal rotation of my hips, resulting in a deformity that would require major hip surgery. Great, another hurdle I had to metaphorically jump!

While I enjoyed going to school, I absolutely dreaded Fridays. Tylden Primary only received enough funding for an integration aide for four days of the week, so every Friday I was sent to a local special school. This was the day when all the students with disabilities from the primary schools in our region went for swimming lessons at the local pool. Swimming was considered an important part of my physiotherapy program, both loosening up my muscles and improving my swimming skills at the same time. And while I enjoyed this part of it, the rest of the day was a nightmare. Most of the other students, who had severe intellectual disabilities, were unable to feed themselves or go to the toilet alone. At lunchtime some students threw their food across the table or made loud, frightening sounds. Their food became missiles that I was forced to duck away from, and the noises they made echoed loudly in my head, scaring me to death.

I was just a 6-year-old, but I vividly remember sitting in my chair with my head down on my arms on the table in front of me. I didn't want to see or hear what was going on around me. It felt like I was in a place I didn't belong and was unable to escape from. The teachers eventually rescued me, seeing how distraught I had become, and took me to another room, away from the other students.

What I hated most about the special school was that, while we all had varying degrees of disabilities, all of the students were treated exactly the same. We were all thrown into the same basket and not identified as individuals with our own, unique personalities or levels of ability or differing needs. It was ironic because usually all I wanted was to be treated the same as the other kids in my class, but on those occasions, as a young boy, I felt strongly that I wasn't one of them, and wanted to be as far away from them as possible. I now understand that they were just like me, probably had similar interests to me, they may have even loved the Collingwood Magpies too, but back then I couldn't see past their often-involuntary actions caused by their disabilities.

The special school operated within a heritage-listed building that dated back to the late 1800's. Just a few years before I became one of its students, children with intellectual disabilities were still living there, institutionalised, many from birth. Just the thought of this makes me sad to think the parents of these children chose to leave their disabled sons and daughters in an institution instead of caring for them at their home. I don't want to sound judgemental, and those parents may have been advised that these decisions were for the best for their children, but I consider myself so lucky that I wasn't left in a corner and abandoned as many disabled children appeared to have been before the 1990's.

Fortunately, by 1993, deinstitutionalisation was well underway and all of the disabled children who had been living at the special school were being placed in the communities of their birthplace. I hope by returning to live with loved ones, if they got that opportunity, that they received the same level of care and attention that I received in my family home.

I hated every single traumatic minute of being a student at that special school, so you can imagine my absolute joy and relief when finally, after four long years my prayers were answered when Mum received a phone call telling her that Tylden Primary had received the funding required to include my physiotherapy there every Friday. When Mum told me that I never had to go back to there again, I nearly fell over, literally! Alleluia! That was the end of an era that, even thinking about now, still fills me with dread.

*

Up until the end of grade three I had been able to walk independently (well, as independently as you can with a walking frame!). It was during grade four when I was nine years old, that I was scheduled to undergo major hip surgery at the RCH. It would be the biggest and most serious surgery I'd ever had, and it would mean recovering at home for several months. But this hospital visit would bring with it one of the most memorable days of my life.

On the morning of the operation, while lying in my hospital bed waiting to be briefed on the day's procedures, I noticed a few familiar, athletic-looking men roaming around the hallways of my ward. I was trying to work out where I had seen their faces before, when Professor Kerr came in to give me and my mum a rundown of what was going to be involved with my surgery.

He said it would take up to six hours and during that time he and his team of surgeons would operate on both of my hips to prevent them from dislocating. Dislocation of the hips is a common problem for people living with cerebral palsy. Due to the tightness in the muscles that connect the hips to the thighbones, the hips often rotate abnormally, causing the ball of the hip to slowly move out of the socket. The surgery to prevent dislocation would involve cutting into my thigh bones and repositioning the ball of the femur back into the hipbone, then metal screws and plates would hold my hips and thighs in their new positions. As well as hip surgery, I was to have my hamstrings and calves operated on to release the tightness in these muscles.

I sometimes fantasised that I was being rebuilt, like Steve Austin from the Six Million Dollar Man back in the 70's. Steve was a fictional astronaut who was injured when his spaceship crashed, prompting the American government to fund the six million dollars it took to rebuild most of his body. When the Six Million Dollar Man awoke, he had superhuman strength and speed. I secretly wished that I would wake from surgery in a new, strong body just like him.

Undergoing surgery was something I embraced, knowing that my parents were making decisions on my behalf that would improve my quality of life by increasing my mobility and decreasing my pain. As agreed with my parents beforehand, I would grin and bear what was coming my way, keeping up my end of the deal to do my best with rehab to recover fully afterwards.

As I was being prepared for surgery, a couple of muscly looking men walked towards my hospital room. I suddenly realised where I recognised the guys from. One of them was Steven Alessio, a ruckman for the Essendon Football Club. I remembered hearing that often high-profile AFL players visited sick children at the RCH as part of the club's community engagement program. These visits were sometimes recorded and reported in the news, but on many occasions, they were private drop-ins, just to put smiles on the faces of young, unwell children.

Well, I thought that this was exciting enough, but when I saw the second guy to wander through the doors, I knew who it was immediately: it was my AFL hero and star player for the Collingwood Magpies, Nathan Buckley.

Steve made his way to my bed and gave me a mini football, trying to remain polite while I unknowingly ignored him; I was so preoccupied with Nathan's presence that I hardly acknowledged poor Steve. By the time Nathan reached my bedside I was starstruck. I froze, totally speechless and felt overawed by his visit. He gave me a Collingwood teddy bear and stayed for a few minutes chatting with my mum, who was also a big Collingwood supporter. I had my photo taken with Nathan and he signed a Collingwood poster for me before saying goodbye and wishing me luck with my surgery.

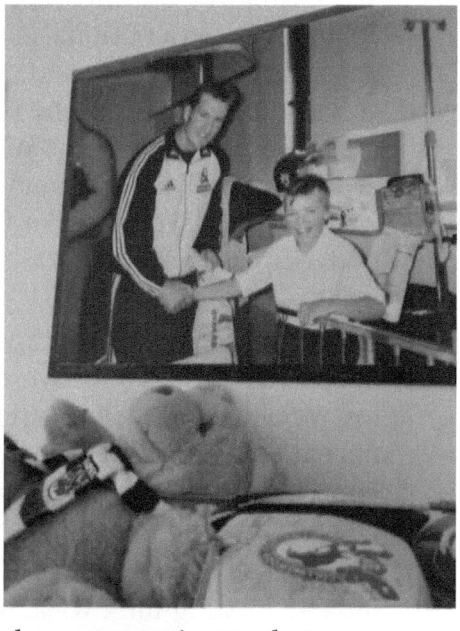

Well, Nathan's visit couldn't have come at a better time as I had forgotten to feel anxious about all the unnatural things they were going to do to my body, and I was wheeled into theatre feeling invincible.

As I counted backwards from 10, my last thoughts before surrendering to the spell of the anaesthetic were about meeting my idol. My grandma knew how much I adored Nathan Buckley and she had been secretly putting calls into the club to see when he was scheduled to visit the hospital. Little did I know that this encounter with

Nathan would be the first of many during our lives, and the beginning of a friendship I would always treasure. The photo of Nathan and me from this first meeting still hangs in my old bedroom at my parents' house in Kyneton and is a reminder of one of the most exciting things that ever happened to me. This meeting with Nathan remains one of the highlights of my life, and he's still my biggest idol!

The surgery was deemed a success and the first part of my recovery involved staying in hospital for a week lying relatively still and being regularly turned by nurses to prevent bedsores. I remember feeling like a turkey on a rotisserie in preparation for the Christmas lunch!

Going home had its challenges for me, too, as well as for my parents, and once at home it became Mum's job to turn the turkey. I had to lie on my back for long periods and Mum had to turn me over every hour to ensure efficient blood circulation.

Teachers and friends from school visited me to help break the boredom, dropping off schoolwork and filling me in on what was happening at school. My grandma popped in often to see how I was getting on and I must have watched my favourite movies, the Lion King and Space Jam, a hundred times! Then after six weeks the hard work of rehabilitation and physiotherapy began, which included numerous trips back and forth to the RCH. Sometimes Mum would buy me a McDonald's Happy Meal as a reward after a gruelling session of having my leg muscles stretched to what almost felt like snapping point. I imagined my hamstrings were like rubber bands and feared that, if pulled too hard, they would split and go flying across the room!

My ultimate aim, one that my parents had always shared, was to stay out of the wheelchair, throw away the Kaye Walker and walk independently. We never took our eyes off the final goal, so physiotherapy had to continue at home where Dad set up a plank in our lounge room that became a critical part of my daily routine. Balance was one of the most important aspects of my recovery and walking in a straight line, back and forth along the plank twice a day, became my challenge. At first, I couldn't even make one length of the plank, and I would cry with the pain of activating my recently operated on hips and hamstrings. Still, I was determined to never give up.

After three long, arduous months, our hard work paid off and I was finally deemed well enough to return to school. Eager to re-join my friends and teachers, I was bursting with excitement to show everyone just how much progress I had made since the surgery. So, at the morning assembly, I stood up in front of the whole school, assisted by my frame, then asked my integration aide, Kerry Cross, to take it away. With my heart thumping hard in my chest, I began by putting one foot in front of the other and walked several metres to the principal. When I finally reached Mr Taylor, who cautiously held out his hands in anticipation of a possible fall, I looked up, eager to learn the reactions of my friends and teachers, and what I saw was overwhelming. All 150 students in that hall were clapping and cheering, while the principal and teachers had tears streaming down their cheeks. All I could do was beam a giant, proud smile. I had defied that doctor who told my parents I would never walk by myself. I was so happy and proud to be able to show off my greatest achievement in nine years. I could walk unassisted for the first time in my life.

*

My newfound walking was put to the test during a grade five school camp at Point Lonsdale, the southern-most tip of Victoria's Bellarine Peninsula. A walking tour up 120 steps to the top of a lighthouse built in 1902 had everybody excited as it was going to be the highlight of our camp. Once at the pinnacle we would be able to look out over Port Phillip Bay, where its rough and choppy seas met the calm waters of Point Lonsdale.

Ms Kerry Cross had been my full-time integration aide at Tylden Primary for the last couple of years and she helped me navigate my way through my early education and learning. Upon discovering our camp destination, Kerry and I calculated that climbing these 120 steps would usually take most people around half an hour. Obviously, I wasn't like most people, but we decided that we were both up for the challenge. So, after weeks of anticipation and excitement, we arrived at camp and set about our journey with great energy and enthusiasm. My wheelchair and Kaye Walker became last resorts for relief when my legs tired from walking, but I still needed assistance with my balance, and began using two metal sticks when walking. These were a godsend during our walk up the lighthouse stairs, which we only realised had no handrails after arriving at the entrance. As I awkwardly manoeuvred one stick and one leg at a time up each step, Kerry and another student followed close behind me, ready to catch me in case I fell backwards. We let the rest of the group pass us and I watched them ascend ever so swiftly ahead of me until I lost sight of them completely. What I wouldn't give to have been able to skip ahead, two and three steps at a time, as my classmates did!

Despite my determination, there were some sections of the winding staircase where Kerry had no choice but to push me from behind, or get in front of me and pull me along. It was clear from the beads of sweat on our foreheads and strained facial expressions that both Kerry and I were being pushed to our limits, both physically and emotionally. Finally, after what felt like the most gruelling hour of my life, we took one final step to the top of the lighthouse staircase where I was blessed to experience one of the most sensational views I'd ever seen. It was one of the greatest senses of achievement I had ever felt.

At the same time that I was trying to inhale the intoxicating view, I was also trying to inhale enough oxygen into my lungs from being so puffed from the strenuous climb. Then, with no warning at all, one of the teachers decidedly announced that it was time to head back down the 120 steps and go back to camp! Exchanging a combined look of both disbelief and acceptance, Kerry and I garnered whatever strength we had left and carefully began the downward journey, this time with her walking in front of me in case I toppled forward. It was as much of an odyssey on the way down as it had been on the way up, but I knew that I could do it (and obviously I had no choice!) so we persevered.

By the end of the lighthouse excursion, I was utterly exhausted but entirely exhilarated. It was an exhausting and challenging climb, but, thankfully, one neither Kerry nor I were prepared to give up on.

I wanted to make it to the top of the lighthouse staircase because I was desperate to see what all the other kids got to see, so that when they talked about everything later, I could be involved in the conversations. I guess you could say that I had a serious case of FOMO as I didn't like being left out, and I certainly wasn't going to let my disability stop me from seeing the same stretch of Port Phillip Bay that my classmates got to experience from that same lookout.

These were the times when I was happiest: when I could experience what other people my age were experiencing. It usually meant that I had to put in much more effort than others, and often had people helping me, but to get to the top of that lighthouse with every other kid on camp meant the world to me. As a ten-year-old my physical abilities were definitely compromised because of my cerebral palsy, but I was learning that being involved in activities with other kids was incredibly rewarding. I still dreamt of becoming an AFL footballer, and while I may never have made it to the big league, little did I know that my dream of playing football in front of a packed stadium would come true sooner than I had expected.

Chapter Five

I'll admit it: I'm one of those annoying Collingwood football supporters that so many people love to hate. Like many Magpie fans, I had no say in which AFL team I was going to barrack for because Mum and her twin brother practically brainwashed me from birth, decking me out in black and white since before I can remember. (Don't worry, this is usual practice for people who love the Collingwood Football Club!) Dad and his family were all Melbourne supporters, so there was always a tug of war over who I should barrack for. But Mum won in the end and I have been a one-eyed Collingwood supporter ever since.

As a child I loved to wear their black and white striped guernsey, I had the scarf and gloves, and my bed was covered with a doona made in the club colours featuring the club mascot, the magpie.

However, as a young boy, I didn't want to just watch football, I wanted to play the game like all the other kids in my town.

It was early in 2001 and I was eleven years old when registrations for Auskick opened in Kyneton. Auskick is an AFL program that introduces young kids to Aussie rules football, where they are taught the basic skills and rules of the game, including how to kick, handball, tackle and shepherd. Once the skills of footy are mastered, usually after a couple of years, players continue their footy careers at a surrounding club in their area. In our case, we chose from the ones that made up the Midland Junior Football League in central Victoria. Kyneton had two teams, South Kyneton and North Kyneton, and I'd already set my sights on playing for the South Kyneton Bombers, because that's the team my friends played for.

I was completely excited at the thought of finally getting the chance to play the game I loved so much. I wasn't going to miss out on my opportunity to sign up, so I'd talked Mum and Dad into taking me to the Kyneton Showgrounds where heaps of kids from school had gathered, decked out in their favourite AFL team colours. Of course, I proudly wore my Collingwood guernsey.

I had the best time playing Auskick and I was treated like everybody else and given opportunities to participate in all the drills at my own pace. Some sessions were spent in the pouring rain in freezing conditions—typical of a Kyneton winter—and on a really cold day it would even snow. My coach at the time, Darryl Sheridan, still says I was always one of the first to turn up for every session and I was always eager to be involved in every drill. I couldn't kick very far or bounce the ball as well as the other kids, but I was doing my best and I was loving every minute of it.

One freezing Saturday, amid much excitement from the Kyneton Auskickers, I was among 20 lucky kids who were given the opportunity to play in a half-time exhibition game during the AFL match between the Carlton Blues and the Freemantle Dockers. As a loud and excited group, we were driven to Melbourne by bus for what was to be an historic game for both the AFL and Auskick. This was to be the first time a player with cerebral palsy was involved in an Auskick exhibition game and, although I didn't know it at the time, breaking new ground for people living with disabilities would form an important part of who I am. The Auskick half-time game became a platform for me which, at the time, generated interest in a child living with a disability that was almost unheard of.

The game was played at Carlton's home ground, Princes Park, and by half-time the Blues were giving the Dockers, the newcomers to the league, an absolute thrashing.

About 15 minutes before we were due to play, we Auskickers were ushered from the grandstand where we had been enthusiastically enjoying the game, down into the players' change rooms where we put on our football boots and started warming up. Like footwear for most sports, footy boots are specially made to grip the oval's surface and make it easier for players to hold their footing in often slippery conditions. But because they didn't make footy boots to fit over my AFO's, I had to play in a pair of my old Blundstone boots. I didn't think much of it at the time, but looking back now, it must have been quite a sight.

Darryl and some of the other coaches were handballing the footy around the group while we jogged on the spot to warm up our legs. I shifted my weight carefully from one leg to the other, eager to limber up for the game. I heard the siren sound signalling half time in the Blues/Dockers game and the crowd cheered their respective AFL heroes off the ground for their break. Butterflies started to dance around in my stomach, knowing it would soon be my turn to run onto the biggest sporting stage I'd play on in my life.

Mum was the only parent allowed in the change rooms as she had helped me get dressed and planned on accompanying me onto the ground, ensuring I had no problems running up the players' race and onto the oval, but the ground officials told her that parents weren't allowed onto the playing surface. Refusing to take no for an answer, Mum politely reminded the officials that my involvement in the game was expected to attract significant media attention which could reflect badly on them if a disabled child's mother was blocked from assisting her son safely onto the playing arena.

They quickly reversed their decision and Mum proudly escorted me up the race and onto the Princes Park playing surface. But our issues didn't end there. The AFL officials had assumed, given my disability, that I was only there to watch the other Auskickers, and ushered me onto the bench. Well, you can imagine Mum's reaction! After just giving them a piece of her mind about her access to the oval, the remaining piece was dished up on a plate to them about shunting me onto the bench.

Again, she was victorious, and I was eventually given the all-clear to join my teammates.

As I clambered onto the ground with my sticks and Blundstones, I imagined I was Nathan Buckley running out onto the hallowed turf at the MCG, proudly showing off his black-and-white-striped guernsey while expertly commanding the oval-shaped ball back and forth from my hand to the grass and back again. Of course, I could only dream of bouncing the ball so that it returned to my hands, which were busy holding onto my metal sticks.

The siren signalled the beginning of our match and as I diligently played the modified game of footy, I could hear the crowd in the grandstands cheering and clapping whenever the ball came near me. I was having so much fun and even managed to score a point for our team, kicking the ball off the ground and dribbling it through the mini posts that had been set up for our game. The crowd went wild when I spoiled a goal for the opposition, as one of my sticks touched the footy that was heading for the goal posts. When the siren sounded and our short match came to an end, the crowd gave me a huge cheer as I wobbled off the ground, so I stopped and raised my sticks in the air to thank them for their support.

Well, anyone would have thought that I'd just run a marathon with the amount of applause I received! Come to think of it, that's probably what it seemed like to those spectators.

I vividly recall an unusual sense of being the centre of attention, being acknowledged in an affirming and positive way, supported by an AFL audience that gathered on Saturday afternoons in their thousands to worship their sporting heroes. Back then, children with disabilities were rarely seen or heard from, so for me to be on the AFL stage in front of a stadium full of enthusiastic spectators was unbelievable.

After the game our main Auskick coach, Kieran McGrath, was interviewed by media personality Rex Hunt on radio station 3AW about the team, but the focus was shifted to the kid with the disability. This was the beginning of a great deal of media interest in my story that I really enjoyed. I suddenly had a newfound interest in a career path of becoming a celebrity!

In the Monday edition of the highest selling newspaper in Melbourne, the Herald Sun, my photo and a story about me was featured on page five. Little did I know that a photographer from the newspaper had captured the moment when I was leaving the ground with my sticks in the air. It was a great shot and really showed how exhilarating it was for me to be out there playing the game I loved. I was clearly thrilled with my latest achievement.

Herald Sun reporter, Natalie Sikora, wrote:

Playing football was something Hayden Walsh used to only dream about. And never did the gutsy boy who suffers from cerebral palsy imagine he would one day play in the

If I can, you can

half-time match at an AFL game. But the 11-year-old's fantasy became a reality at the weekend when Hayden hit the turf with his friends during the Carlton-Fremantle clash at Optus Oval "I feel fantastic," Hayden said yesterday from his Kyneton home. "I didn't think I would make it. There were about 50 kids and only 20 got to go. I couldn't believe it at first." Hayden, who joined Auskick for the first time this year, said he was nervous when he first made his way onto the field during Saturday's game. But the crowd made him feel on top of the world. Even more of a thrill was that he kicked a point! "Just being out there on a big ground made me feel great," he said. "I just kept up with the other guys and stayed with my opponent." What the youngster, who was diagnosed with cerebral palsy at 13 months of age, did not expect was the crowd reception he received when he walked off the field. "They all stood up and started cheering. I just thought they were clapping for the other team, but they were clapping for me. It was unbelievable." "I just put my sticks up in the air to say thank-you. They made me feel so special." Hayden said it had been his lifelong dream to play footy, but his condition had made it almost impossible. "I just love football. I never thought I would really play," he said. "I really wished when I was a little boy that I could play football. On Saturday I achieved it. I still can't believe it." Watching from the sidelines, his proud mother, Coral, was almost in tears at the sheer joy of seeing her son play. After a series of operations for his condition, Mrs Walsh said she never thought she would see the day when Hayden would be up and running, let alone kicking a footy. Signing up Hayden to play was a big injury risk. But yesterday the overwhelmed mother said it was well worth it. "It was just amazing, I'm so proud," said Mrs Walsh. "It felt amazing." Hayden said he didn't let his condition get him down. "It hasn't stopped me. I just love sport and I love being involved with it. It makes me feel fantastic just to have fun with my friends."

The following Friday I was featured in the Macedon Ranges' Guardian newspaper with the story's caption being, "HAYDEN GRABS THE HEADLINES". How true that was! I was photographed with coach Darryl handpassing the footy and Darryl had told the newspaper, "*Hayden handpasses from either side of his body, is capable of taking a strong chest mark and overhead mark, and he can kick the ball off the ground. The only problem is there are no football boots suitable for Hayden's callipers, so he plays in Blundstones!*" My unorthodox footy boots were front and centre in the photo in our local newspaper, and while the coach was accurate in his description of my footwear, he was particularly generous about my marking abilities!

I was awarded the Junior Sports Star of the Week and received a forty-dollar gift voucher from the Kyneton Surf Shop. Surfing wasn't high on my list of endeavours, but fortunately they sold cool t-shirts and caps, so I spent my voucher on them.

The following week a camera crew and journalist from *Channel 7 News* came to my primary school and filmed me playing footy on the oval, as well as interviewing me about the Auskick game. Not long after that story went to air, Channel 7's rival network, Channel 9, organised an interview with me to be filmed live on the *Sunday Footy Show*. The Channel 9 media truck parked outside our house while the cameramen set up inside our lounge room. For me, it felt like we were on the set of a Hollywood blockbuster! I was dressed in my Tylden Primary school uniform, and when it was time to be interviewed, I sat on the couch in front of the camera with Mum, Darryl and his three sons Taylor, Mitch and Morgan. Dad was working, but I think that suited him just fine as appearing on national TV was not something he ever wanted to do. I sure felt pumped and was loving all the publicity I was getting. The journalist told me to turn on my cheeky smile for the cameras and then we were on air. Mum agreed to be interviewed, but she was uncomfortable and left most of the speaking to Darryl and myself. However, she did speak of how proud she and Dad were of the progress I had made since my major surgery the previous year, while Darryl told the journalist how determined I was to play the game I loved, with high spirits and a great sense of fun.

After they had finished filming, the Channel 9 journalist got chatting with my Mum and was interested in the types of treatments I was undergoing at the Children's Hospital to help my mobility. Within weeks, I featured in another Channel 9 story and this time it was a health report based around a new trial I was involved in at the RCH's Gate Laboratory under the guidance of my orthopaedic surgeon, Professor Kerr.

During this trial, little black balls were placed around my body and used as a way of mapping my range of movements as I walked along a black line. An image resembling a skeleton was reflected onto a big screen and it was like a life-size puzzle of join the dots. I had lots of fun, pretending to kick a soccer ball and handpass a Sherrin football, providing great visuals for the news crew. They also interviewed Professor Kerr, Mum and me, and that night my one-and-a-half-minute story went to air. Again, I was elated, convinced that my road to celebrity was going to be a smooth one.

At the end of 2001 Professor Kerr won the *John Mitchell Crouch Fellowship*, the highest research award from the Royal Australasian College of Surgeons. I felt proud to have been involved in the trials and hoped they would one day help me and other children living with CP to move more freely.

When I got back to school on the Monday following my round of media appearances, everybody wanted to be my friend, including the kids who I thought hated me! It was a wonderful feeling and one that I wasn't familiar with, so I enjoyed it while it lasted and even signed several autographs. Some kids said I was blowing up their televisions and wondered when I would get the call up to star in *Home and Away*. Funnily enough, I'm still waiting for that call, but I remember feeling strangely comfortable in front of the cameras and secretly hoped my media stardom would continue forever. I even thought I might have been offered some modelling opportunities too, considering that I had been such a gorgeous baby, after all. But unfortunately, my services were not required there, either. Yet.

Thankfully though, I have noticed over the past few years that large retailers like *Target* have begun casting children who use wheelchairs and Kaye Walkers as models for their clothes. This type of inclusivity is so refreshing and sends positive messages about people who live with disabilities. The children featured in the ads look happy and I hope they feel great self-worth. For many years the only types of advertisements that featured people living with disabilities were associated with victims of car accidents, which created a negative stereotype. It is great to see that the lives of people like me, who live with disability, are valued and represented across all sectors of our communities, from sport to politics and everything in between.

Not long after my introduction to stardom, my parents were contacted by a couple in Melbourne whose daughter was my age and also lived with cerebral palsy.

They had been inspired by my story and wanted their daughter to meet me.

Our parents organised a meeting in Kyneton and we began having regular catchups where she and I would go swimming in the new indoor pool at Gisborne or have lunch at the Country Cob Bakery in Kyneton's main street. (Their award-winning pies were just as delicious then as they are now!) I felt I had been able to help another child and another family deal with their cerebral palsy journey and that made me feel good.

To cap off a great 2001, I was nominated by the South Kyneton Football Club (SKFC) to be the prince in the annual Kyneton Daffodil Parade. The Football Club had invited me to train and play with them after the Auskick season had finished that year and they surprised me by putting my name up as their choice for the 2001 Parade prince. It was an annual tradition for two adults to be selected as the parade's king and queen, while children were chosen as the prince and princesses. In the weeks leading up to the parade we had to have publicity photos taken wearing our regalia at *Myer* in Bendigo for the local newspapers. The princess wore blue, while the queen and king both wore special gowns and crowns. As the prince I wore a green cape and a matching green cap, which made me feel like a superhero. But at the same time, I began to realise that I didn't need superpowers to help me feel great and to achieve, I was doing that by just being me and people were starting to notice the boy who lived with cerebral palsy.

On the day of the Daffodil Parade, it was overcast and chilly but thousands of Kynetonians turned out, lining the footpaths of the main street. The procession of floats included loads of community groups like kindergartens, schools, sporting clubs and musical bands. As parade monarchs we rode in the Lions Club's miniature train where we waved and smiled, while our families and friends proudly waved back. It was a great honour for me to be chosen as the prince as it was the first time a person with a disability had ever been selected to be a monarch in the parade's 47-year history. Who would have thought? A royal with a disability!

The magnitude of my participation during the Daffodil Parade feels more significant to me now than it did back then; it was another big step in the right direction for inclusivity of people living with disability. If other kids with additional needs saw me up there as the prince, then they, too, could see what was possible for them. I hope I had a positive impact on at least one other child that day.

It appeared that many others wanted to ride on the back of my celebrity, too, so there were more media opportunities after the parade, making my eleventh year definitely one to remember!

Life soon got back to normal following my fifteen minutes of fame, and after a year in Auskick I decided I had learnt enough and was ready to play competitive junior football. I had been pestering Darryl for months and finally convinced him to approach Mum and Dad for their permission for me to play for the South Kyneton Junior Football Club. My parents thought it was dangerous for me to play footy at that level and worried that I would get injured, but like all of my endeavours, they have always been behind me one hundred per cent and eventually agreed to let me sign up.

Darryl appointed me to be his Under 11's assistant coach and let me help him choose the teams and participate in training, but I wasn't allowed to play in the Saturday games against other clubs. It made me feel sad that I was singled out and excluded from weekend games when I trained every Tuesday and Thursday with the rest of the team each week after school. I let Darryl know how unhappy I was and told him that all I wanted to do was play competitive footy like everybody else. My motto was, 'I just want to do what they're doing'. I didn't think it was too much to ask.

I must have worn Darryl down with my weekly pestering, because eventually he gave in and, as the league delegate, agreed to take my case to the Midland Junior Football League meeting for consideration. He promised he would do his best to fight for me in the hopes that we would get the green light so I could run out with my team and compete during home and away games.

From all accounts, the discussion at the League meeting was a robust one and Darryl was asked to put forward evidence to demonstrate why I should be allowed to play with South Kyneton because, physically, I was still relying on my sticks to help me walk and my lower legs were supported with AFO's. I had demonstrated to Darryl at training that I could run without my sticks, albeit slowly, and I could kick a ball along the ground, but some League officials had concerns about me being injured during competitive games. Darryl had a strong argument that, legally, the League could neither discriminate against, nor exclude me from games because of my disability. Thankfully, somebody on my side, fighting for my rights! At the ripe old age of 13 I was becoming a trailblazer for people with disabilities without even knowing it! It took a couple of further meetings, but Darryl suggested a compromise that was voted on and finally accepted by the League.

It was agreed that I would be listed on the team sheet and I was allowed to participate in games for ten minutes during the second half, with Darryl to accompany me onto the ground and supervise my participation in the game. The plan was to position me in the forward pocket with the expectation that the ball wasn't going to enter that section of the ground too often. But as Darryl puts it, I was like a ball magnet! The moment I entered the ground with him, the footy would magically end up near me. Supporters would scream from the boundary, "Go Hayden!", and "Kick it, Hayden!", and most times I managed to scramble to the ball and kick it off the ground. Darryl later recalled, "Hayden's legs and sticks were going everywhere but there was no stopping him, he desperately wanted to play football and it made him feel 10-feet tall."

I realised then that I'd found a real ally in coach Darryl, and if it hadn't been for him, I may not ever have had the opportunity to play Australian rules football. Darryl understood my yearning to be involved and participate in sport like the other kids in the town. He had great empathy for me as he, too, had experienced what it was like to be disabled, albeit for a short period of time.

Darryl had been struck down by a disabling condition just a couple of years earlier and had almost lost his legs. He had contracted meningococcal meningitis, a bacterial form of meningitis which causes a serious infection of the lining that surrounds the brain and spinal cord. Fifty percent of people who contract meningococcal meningitis die from the disease.

While Darryl was in hospital in a coma, his legs turned black from his knees down to his ankles, as did his arms from his elbows to his fingertips. He could have lost all four limbs, or even worse, he could have died. But amazingly, with numerous rounds of antibiotics and ongoing prayers from his family and community, he made a full and remarkable recovery.

I will always be indebted to him for helping me achieve my childhood dream of playing football with the other kids at my club.

Unfortunately for me, however, my playing days were short lived.

By the time I was 12 and playing Under 13's football, the size and strength of the other players meant that it was becoming dangerous for me to be involved in games. I wasn't a tall boy and my parents' concerns that I would be injured were intensifying so, against my wishes, it was decided that I would no longer play footy. I was devastated by this decision and felt that I was being babied and wrapped up in cotton wool. All I wanted was to be like the other kids and play the game I loved. But, at the end of the day, I had to abide by my parents' decisions as they knew what was best for me. I was relegated to being the Under 13's assistant coach and handing out oranges for the players during weekend matches.

However, little did I know that almost 20 years later I would be allowed to pull on the Kyneton Tigers' guernsey again and be given a taste of what it feels like to run out with my team to play footy, representing my beloved club once more.

Chapter Six

I was devastated to learn at the end of grade six that the teachers had made the decision to keep me in primary school for what turned out to be another two years. The teachers deemed that because of the amount of school I had missed due to medical appointments, surgery and rehabilitation at home, I wasn't adequately prepared to graduate to secondary school, at least in an academic sense. I would need to stay on and improve my reading and writing and develop a better understanding of basic mathematical functions before I could begin year seven.

Frustratingly, this was one of the decisions being made on my behalf that I had no control over, nor could I change. I just had to grin and bear it. So, when I finally graduated from primary school, I was 13 years old and would turn 14 in the May of my first secondary school year.

I began year 7 at Sacred Heart Secondary College, Kyneton, in 2004, the same school my aunties and grandmother had attended decades earlier.

Unlike Tylden Primary where the landscape was largely flat, at Sacred Heart there were three multistorey buildings with upper-level classrooms that were only accessible by stairs. The school was built on a large hill that spanned from the college's front entrance to the football oval at the rear of the property. In between there was a steep descent, with the fall broken by several sets of stairs and a long driveway. As you could imagine, this made it very difficult for me to get around quickly and easily on my own.

I was, however, given an old blue electric scooter to drive around school for a while, until my physiotherapist received some funds through Scope and bought me a brand new one, enabling me to ditch the old blue bomb! The scooter made it easier to get up and down steep hills, but the teachers were forever reprimanding me for driving too fast. Other students sometimes took my scooter for a spin, usually landing us all in trouble.

My scooter stayed at school and my favourite mode of transport for getting to and from school was my red three-wheeler trike. The owners of the local toyshop had imported the trike which was an adult version of a three-wheeler some young children learn to ride before they advance to a bicycle with training wheels. I rode as a young boy. My trike was a gift from my parents for my twelfth birthday and it was my pride and joy. It gave me my first taste of true independence as I left home every morning without having to rely on anyone to get me there. My school bag fitted neatly into a large basket that sat between the two back wheels and a loud bell was attached to the front handlebars and I wasn't afraid to use it if anybody got in my way.

Around the same time, I was given a Sony Walkman, the old-fashioned way of listening to music with earphones attached to a small cassette holder that I attached to my belt around my waist. I thought I was the coolest kid on the block listening to my favourite tunes from the Pet Shop Boys. Nobody had to pull me or push me, my feet sat comfortably on the pedals and I exerted just enough pressure to propel myself to my destination. Nothing could compare to the freedom I felt while riding my trike as I sang along to 'Go West' on my daily journey to school.

Like most typical teenage boys though, I took risks and rode too fast, dodging and weaving in and out of the foot traffic, quickly earning a reputation as a speed demon.

My favourite place at Sacred Heart was the sports oval. It was there at lunchtimes that I joined my mates to play footy and it was my happy place where I was accepted as a footballer, just one of the boys.

My mates still think it's hysterical now when they recall one day when we were having a kick and I suddenly fell over in the middle of the oval. The ball was nowhere near me, neither were any other kids, but I just suddenly fell flat on my face, my arms hitting the ground first before I faceplanted onto the wet grass. Some of the lads ran over to help me up, thinking I'd been injured or something. Then when I was back on my feet again and they asked what happened, I told them that a strong gust of wind knocked me over. They all suddenly fell over too, and I thought that something very strange was going on. Then I realised that they had fallen over from laughing their heads off at the thought of a sudden, invisible gust of wind on a perfectly still day knocking me off my feet!

At the time I laughed too, but to this day I still believe there was a freak gust of wind that pushed me over. My memory generally serves me well, so that's the story I'm sticking with!

Making my way back to class from the oval after recess and lunch was often one of my biggest challenges and felt like I was competing in a marathon. Sometimes if, for one reason or another I wasn't driving my scooter, I got caught out with just my sticks down on the oval. On these occasions I would usually begin the long journey back to class, ages before the other students, who enjoyed every last second of their freedom before quickly gathering any items they'd brought outside with them and racing back to class at the sound of the bell, overtaking me on the way.

Like most new kids going into year seven, it was like starting school all over again, going from primary school where you were the biggest, oldest and toughest (well, I was mentally tough, if nothing else), to being the youngest, smallest and most vulnerable.

Even though I was older than most of the others in year seven, I wasn't tall, and I blended in well with the boys and girls who were up to two years younger than me. The only obvious difference between us was my cerebral palsy.

Only a handful of students from my old primary school began year seven at Sacred Heart with me, but there was one very familiar face I was happy to see every day. Jenny O'Brien had been my integration aide in Prep at Tylden, and I'd known her for my entire eight years at primary school. She successfully applied for the job as my integration aide at Sacred Heart and we became a great team.

A highlight of my first year at Sacred Heart was a visit to the school by Jim Asimakopoulos, a man who lived with cerebral palsy.

Jim's story was amazing, and I was enthralled at how he had lived his life. He was born in 1988 and for his first six months had been on life support to keep him alive. He didn't learn how to speak until he was 12 years old, and decades later he made his living from speaking to school children and sporting clubs about life with CP. Jim spoke to our year level about how people with disabilities were 'people first', and continued to do so every year until I was in year nine. Jim was employed by the Victorian Education Department when he convinced then Education Minister, Joan Kirner, that he could have a positive influence on children and their attitudes to people living with disabilities. Jim went on to deliver over seven thousand workshops, speaking to over one hundred and seventy-five thousand children at schools and sporting clubs across Victoria. His CP was more severe than mine, he was a wheelchair user and his language was difficult to understand, but he inspired me and gave me hope. I loved hearing about his life and his positive attitude to living with a disability. He told us he wouldn't swap his cerebral palsy for anything in the world, he was happily married and he didn't want to be what most people considered 'normal'; he just wanted to be Jim. He suggested to our year level that when they met a person living with a disability, instead of asking them what was wrong with them, to ask them what they are able to do. He also had a good sense of humour and, because he barracked for Richmond, he had a dig at me for following the Magpies!

I felt I had a lot in common with Jim and that I could relate to him. His visits to Sacred Heart during my first three years were some of the happiest days I had at school.

Jim became another idol of mine as he created opportunities for himself and fought to achieve his goals. In doing so he raised awareness of CP and, more importantly, began to change the attitudes school children had in relation to disabilities.

Jim was rewarded for his efforts in 2006 when he received a Queen's Birthday Order of Australia for services to people with disabilities as an advocate, through raising public awareness and promoting the benefits of integrated education in the community.

I thought back then that maybe one day, I too, could speak to school children or other community groups about the real-life experiences of people living with a disability. They might be surprised at just how similar our lives all are!

Whilst there were many high points to my life at secondary school, one of my biggest disappointments was not being allowed to participate in the year nine Murray River camp. This was the camp that ran over several days and nights and included river rafting, hiking and setting up and packing down camp sites each morning and night. It sounded like so much fun and I would have given my left leg to have been allowed to go on that camp (not that anyone would have wanted my left leg, I suppose).

The school made the decision that it would be too dangerous for me to go rafting down the Murray, Australia's longest river which runs through three states. The year nine co-ordinator also felt that my mobility issues meant that it would be too hard for me to hike to each destination then be responsible for putting up my own tent and camp for the night. I remember thinking, "Here we go again; another decision made for me that I have no power to change!"

Jenny was desperate to try to get me on the camp and suggested we be allowed to take a caravan on the trip, which would enable me to travel by road to each destination, meet up with the rest of the group and then sleep in the van. However, her suggestions were rejected 'for safety reasons' and to protect me from accidents. It was recommended that Jenny use the money that had been budgeted for my place on the camp and take me and Jack Simpson, a student who lived with epilepsy and wasn't allowed to go either, on an urban camp to Melbourne's CBD.

Reluctantly accepting this as the next best substitute, Jack and I were given the task of choosing and planning the activities we wanted to partake in during our time in the Big Smoke. On reflection, I can see how this was a great exercise in learning how to plan and stick to a budget, as we could only use the money that we had been allocated. We had to organise our own accommodation, restaurants and admission tickets, and we practised making phone calls to Jenny's husband and our parents so that when the time came, we were confident enough to pick up the phone and make the bookings.

I chose for us to go to the museum and watch a movie on the 3D screen. Jack and I were really excited about being able to experience something in 3D, which almost made us feel a little bit superior to the other kids who were no doubt battling with wind and rain while setting up their tents every night. Unfortunately, this ended up being a frightening experience for us. The movie was about sharks and, as is the nature of 3D images, the entire picture seemed as though they literally leapt from the screen right onto us, scaring us half to death. Jack and I were so terrified we almost ended up in Jenny's lap! Ironically, as it turned out, my visit to the sharks at Melbourne's Aquarium many years later was one of the most significant days of my life.

Jack's choice of activity was to go and see the live performance of the *Lion King* at the Regent Theatre. We thought this was pretty exciting as it was the first time either of us had experienced a live show. I loved it because I'd seen the movie so many times and I could sing along with my favourite songs, like 'Hakuna Matata' and 'Can you Feel the Love Tonight?' and I knew the characters and storyline inside out.

We had selected our accommodation in Carlton, just a block away from the famous Lygon Street strip, which is full of traditional Italian restaurants, pizzerias, cafes and gelati shops.

Neither Jack nor I had ever been to Lygon Street before; we were wide-eyed kids from the country enjoying our first taste of what some referred to as 'Little Italy'. Waiters stood at the entrance to their restaurants with smiles on their faces and menus tucked under their arms, trying to lure us into their eateries, but we politely bypassed, intent on keeping our booking with a pizzeria renowned for making the best pizzas in town.

As we entered the restaurant, Jenny tilted the front of my wheelchair slightly to avoid a small step, before finding our table. We had decided to use the wheelchair that evening, after an exhausting day of walking and travel. Once I was comfortably seated, my wheelchair was tucked away in a corner and I sat next to Jack and Jenny at a table covered with a red and white checked cloth. Little green, white and red flags had been placed in the middle of the table symbolising Italy's colours, alongside serviettes and plastic flowers in a small vase.

Well, we were glad we chose this restaurant because the pizzas were magnificent! I'd ordered one with the lot and you can guess the mess I made of myself with my crooked fingers juggling the large triangular slab I'd picked up as melted cheese and slices of salami started sliding off the side. After our meal an older Italian gentleman, who we learnt was the restaurant owner, was doing the rounds of his customers' tables when he stopped to chat with Jack and me.

He had a strong Italian accent and asked us how we enjoyed the pizzas before offering us a gelati, "On the house". I chose my favourite combination of chocolate and peppermint, and it didn't disappoint! At the end of our first major city trip, Jack and I agreed that the urban camp was a great experience, and we didn't feel like we'd missed out on much, not being with the other kids along the Murray

River. I actually felt lucky that I had a comfortable bed in the heated Carlton apartment, while the other campers would have been in a cold tent on the hard ground in their sleeping bags.

There was another year nine urban camp that Jack and I were allowed to be a part of which was the 'Amazing Race Around Melbourne'. Essentially, students were put into teams and given a list of clues about various city locations, like the museum, the art gallery and Parliament House. The students had to use their geography and map-reading skills to determine the best way of getting there, either by tram, train or sometimes running. The first team to prove they'd been to each of the landmarks won the race.

However, disappointingly for us, instead of being teamed up with the other kids in our year level, Jack and I had to form 'teams' with our integration aide again. This annoyed me because, as much as I liked Jack and Jenny, I wanted to be involved with my other mates like everyone else was. Still, I thought it was better than not going at all, and I knew I would meet up with everyone at the accommodation at the end of each day.

In order to meet each challenge, we used public transport to get around the city, and to speed up the process I agreed to leave my sticks at the apartment and be pushed in my wheelchair.

This turned into a near disaster when I was left seated on the tram alone after Jenny and Jack got off ahead of me, taking my wheelchair with them. The intention was for them to get off first with my chair and then help me off the tram before it continued on with the rest of its journey. Instead, the tram driver had seen them get off the tram, assumed that my wheelchair belonged to Jack, and accelerated slowly towards the next tram stop with me on board. I was petrified and froze in my seat, not knowing what to do.

A lady sitting opposite me saw what was happening and tried to get the driver's attention by knocking on the window that separated him from the passengers. It wasn't until Jenny started banging on the side of the tram for him to stop that he realised something was wrong. He halted and opened the doors, enabling Jenny to come back onto the tram and help me off, which was lucky because I would have spent the rest of the afternoon circling around Melbourne by myself in an old red rattling tram!

Jenny and I certainly shared some interesting experiences together and she was the person I felt most comfortable with, enough to confide in her at a time during year nine when I'd had enough of school. I'd been finding my studies difficult and I just wasn't enjoying being there, and I told her I wanted to leave school and get into the workforce.

That's when she came up with her clever plan.

Sacred Heart had been undergoing some construction work with an extension being added onto one of its buildings. She organised with the site manager for me to join the brick laying crew and be put on 'wheelbarrowing sand duties'. I was excited to be able to experience what it was like to be in the workforce and turned up at school ready to work—not to learn—in my Blundstones and flannelette shirt. The site manager played along with Jenny's ingenious plan, leading me to a pile of sand on the ground, then plonked a heavy wheelbarrow and shovel in front of me. He instructed me to shovel the sand from the ground into the wheelbarrow, then, once full, take the wheelbarrow to the bricklayers at the cement mixer about forty metres away.

Enthusiastically, I discarded my sticks, replacing them with the shovel and got to work.

My first challenge was getting a good grip on the shovel, as my fingers couldn't quite make it around the handle. But I did my best, then, leaning in on the shovel as I pushed it into the sand, I transferred it into the wheelbarrow. It must have taken thirty shovels of sand to even cover the base of the wheelbarrow, and by this stage I was sweating heavily. Another worker on the site encouraged me, telling me I was doing a good job and suggested that I only half-fill the wheelbarrow as it might get too heavy to push if it was completely full. I thanked him for his advice and continued for another half an hour until I had my first half wheelbarrow load.

Pushing it to the concrete mixer was the next challenge, and not one I enjoyed. Awkwardly, I grabbed hold of the wheelbarrow handles and began wobbling the heavy load towards the concrete mixer. I was really struggling and almost tipped the wheelbarrow a couple of times before I got to my destination. By this stage I was seriously doubting whether I was cut out to be a bricklayer, but I managed to move a couple more loads of sand before the site manager signalled a morning tea break.

Jenny joined us for morning tea, and while I told her it was hard yakka, I said I'd continue to work for as long as I could. I lasted another few loads, then it was agreed that I call it a day. My clothes were wet through with sweat, my body was aching, and fatigue had set in; I definitely wasn't cut out to be a brickie.

I was disappointed how this work experience ended, but I knew I'd given it all I had, and that wasn't enough. My body wasn't strong enough for the physical labour required to be a bricklayer, or any labourer.

The next day Jenny and I discussed my education, agreeing that I would continue at school and she would help me seek out some work experience that I was more suited to.

In her own way, Jenny had proven how important an education was for me, and that I would need to use my brain, not only my muscles, when I eventually entered the workforce.

That same year a new girl named Morgan, who was also a wheelchair user, began at Sacred Heart in year seven, and I felt it was my responsibility as a year nine student with a disability to keep an eye out for her.

In the beginning, nobody from her year level sat with her at recess or lunchtime so I began meeting Morgan between classes to try to make her feel a little more welcome. She had a very rare condition called congenital disorder of glycosylation (CDG), which affects the muscles. She was unable to walk or stand on her own and her speech was very difficult to understand. To help her communicate she used a Lightwriter, a small device that translated her speech into text, similar to the one used by Professor Stephen Hawking, the English physicist who developed motor neurone disease when he was just 21.

It didn't take long before Morgan and I developed a friendship and started hanging out together. We did most of the usual things that kids our age did, like going to the movies and visiting each other's houses. She lived on a property a few kilometres out of Kyneton where she indulged in her great love of riding horses. And I don't just mean any horses, I mean big, equestrian horses! I usually watched her riding from outside the arena they had at their house. While Morgan rode, I would daydream, wondering about how she felt up there, high off the ground, as high as branches in nearby trees where birds nested with their offspring. I wondered what it would be like to be so free, to rely on no other person, but instead trust a large, four-legged animal to navigate its way around the open-air arena, then enable its rider to safely return to ground level.

Then one day I built up the courage to ask if I could have a ride, too. Mum and Dad would never have approved, but as they weren't there, I went for it. I was very nervous, as I'd only ever been on one of those gentle pony rides along St Kilda's Esplanade where you're slowly walked along while the docile pony is guided with a rope. This was one of my many treasured memories from the regular visits to my cousins' house in Brighton.

At Morgan's property a ramp had been built on the edge of the riding arena, enabling her to push herself in her wheelchair up to a flat platform where she could then be helped onto her horse that stood next to her, and off she would go, riding like it was second nature to her. To prevent her falling forward in her saddle, she wore a brace fitted around here torso that helped keep her upright.

When it came to my turn, using my sticks I was able to stagger up the ramp to the platform. Morgan's mum helped me into the saddle, and I remember being very scared as I was so high up off the ground, but at the same time I was excited and proud that I was trying something new. Sitting on top of a full-sized equestrian horse put me almost two metres off the ground and whilst my

body was shaking like a leaf, my sweaty hands gripping as tightly as they could to the reigns, I felt incredible as I was lead around the arena by Morgan's mum, who made sure the ride was gentle so as not to aggravate my hips and tight hamstrings, and naturally also ensuring that I didn't fall off!

Morgan was an amazing athlete and competitor and went on to join Equestrian Australia, competing successfully in the *Federation Equestre Internationale Para Dressage* as a classified 1A rider, the highest level of physical impairment. Her dream was to represent Australia at the Paralympics, and with her attitude, I always believed she would. In 2013 the Horsezone magazine published a story about Morgan, quoting a saying she said she lived by.

Tell me it can't be done
and I will do it.
Tell me the goal is too high
and I will reach it.
Place an obstacle in front of me
and I will soar over it.
Challenge me, dare me, or even defy me.
But do not underestimate me.
For on the back of my horse
Anything is possible.

ANON

While living with my own disability, I have always been interested in the stories of others who also have additional needs, both cognitive and physical.

I'd spent a lot of time at Sacred Heart with Jack Simpson, and while I got to know him pretty well, it was Jenny who told me about his amazing health journey.

Jack had lived without disability until the age of eight when, in 1999, he suffered a serious epileptic seizure. Jack was eventually diagnosed with multiple sclerosis, blood cancer and epilepsy, as well as the loss of neurological functions. Practically overnight he became a wheelchair user, unable to carry out the most basic of daily tasks. After being disappointed with many different treatment options that weren't suitable for him at the time, it seemed that only a miracle could give him back his life. And some believe that that's exactly what happened.

One freezing winter's night in August 2000, while Jack's mum, Sharon, was putting him into bed, she felt the warm touch of a woman, fully dressed in a brown nun's habit, gently helping her to lift him from his wheelchair into his bed. Shocked and in disbelief, but extremely grateful for the help, Sharon believed with every part of her being that this was an apparition of the catholic nun, Sister Mary MacKillop, who died in August 1909.

On a second occasion, Mary MacKillop again appeared kneeling by his bed, praying.

Within three years of the onset of Jack's illnesses, he began to recover and by the end of 2002 parishioners at St Ambrose Catholic Church in Woodend witnessed Jack walking by himself, appearing to have completely recovered.

His neurologist, Dr Andrew Kornberg from the Royal Children's Hospital, told the Catholic Weekly magazine, *"The treatment for the multiple sclerosis and lymphoma may account for the healings there, but what is so unexpected has been the recovery of brain function."*

By this stage there was a strong movement underway to have Mary MacKillop canonised and for her to become Australia's first saint. Jack's recovery didn't end up being the catalyst for Mary's canonisation by Pope Benedict XVI in Rome in October 2010, but anybody who knew Jack and his story believed there'd definitely been a miracle.

From time-to-time friends and colleagues have asked me if I ever wished that it were me who was cured by a miracle. My answer has changed from wishing it was me when I was a young boy, but now as an adult I no longer want to be anyone else other than myself, the way I am, complete with my disability. In fact, looking back now, I feel incredibly lucky that I only have CP, and didn't have to endure the multiple medical conditions that Jack did. I remember one day when I was in the school library when I looked up the definition of cerebral palsy and read that there is no cure, yet. Soon after that I asked Mum why God chose me to have cerebral palsy and she responded with, "Hayden, you were given the life you have, and it's up to you to make the most of it." That's what I am doing; living with the body I was given to the best of my ability.

Chapter Seven

The Queen once described one of the worst years of her life as an 'annus horribilis'. That was 1992 when scandal rocked the British royal family with multiple marriage breakdowns. My annus horribilis was 2007.

I was seventeen years old and in year ten. Some of my friends already had girlfriends, and they helped me make up my mind to also explore new relationships with girls. Back then, just before things like Instagram and Facebook took over the social media scene, we used a social networking platform called *Myspace* to connect with friends online. It was very similar to Facebook and enabled users to upload photos and videos, connect with friends and send private messages. Just like Facebook, it was very popular with teenagers and within weeks I had accumulated three hundred *Myspace* friends. I proudly displayed a photo of myself with my sticks that clearly showed my disability. But when I tried to start conversations online with a few girls online they all cut me off. Clearly my disability was something they couldn't deal with and weren't willing to give me a chance. This made me sad.

Most of my *Myspace* friends were teenagers from the Macedon Ranges who either went to school at Sacred Heart, Kyneton High School or Braemar College, a private school on Mount Macedon. Many of them I had never met, including a girl called Lauren. But my mate Matt Dettman knew her and thought we'd get on well so suggested that I reach out to her through *Myspace*.

I took his advice and Lauren accepted my friend request almost immediately! The very next day, sitting at my computer with fingers poised over the keyboard, I found the courage to send her a private message asking her how she was and which football team she barracked for. After school the following day I nervously logged onto my computer and to my delight, Lauren had responded. I learnt that she barracked for the Western Bulldogs, formerly called the Footscray Football Club. From Lauren's profile photo, I could see that she was a pretty girl with long dark hair and a slender, athletic looking figure. I was excited that she was taking an interest in me and freely contributing to our online chats every couple of nights. To my great relief, my disability didn't put her off like it did the others, and she sent me a surprise *Myspace* happy birthday wish on my birthday, which made me feel very special.

We continued our regular online chats, but moved from *Myspace* to the MSN Messenger platform, as I'd heard of hackers breaking into people's *Myspace* accounts and spreading their private information. I didn't want anybody knowing about my online relationship with Lauren, except for my two closest mates, Matt and Damien. I wanted to keep it private, a secret, especially from my parents.

Lauren and I had been chatting online for a couple of months and I was beginning to like her more and more and really hoped that I'd have the chance to meet her. I knew that if we could meet in person I could then gauge if she 'like-liked' me, and if she would give me a chance to be her boyfriend.

My opportunity soon came around when Matt invited me to a party at a farm property in a nearby district. I hadn't been to a party as a teenager before and was extremely nervous. But I was determined to go, and got dressed up in my favourite outfit, my best blue jeans, a nice shirt and my favourite jumper. I'd been shaving once a week for a few months, so I also scraped away the miniscule amount of stubble on my chin before dabbing on a generous amount of Dad's Tabac Eau de Cologne. I didn't tell my parents about the party, but just that I was going out with the boys. So, when Dad drove me to Matt's house, while he didn't ask, he must have wondered why I'd gone to the effort of making myself smell and look so good! I had dressed to impress and was excited about meeting Lauren, but that would have to wait as the boys were first sculling pre's at Matt's house (you know, having drinks somewhere first, before arriving at the party). I decided to stick to soft drinks until I got to the party, as I knew that just two or three alcoholic drinks would further compromise my mobility. I didn't want to be stumbling in under the influence before I had a chance to make a good first impression on Lauren!

When we were dropped off at the party there were people everywhere: groups standing inside the house, others on the back verandah, and more standing around a fire burning in a rusted old 44-gallon drum. I'd studied Lauren's appearance from her profile picture and was sure that the girl standing with a group of her friends in the backyard was unmistakably her. Gripping hold of my sticks tighter than usual, I walked up to the group of girls who, upon seeing me, quickly disbanded, leaving Lauren and I awkwardly alone. It was so nice being able to meet her in person and she was just as pretty as her profile picture. We spoke for about ten minutes and during that time, while nervous, I felt surprisingly comfortable talking about school and our football teams, and I told her about an operation I was going to be having on my feet and hips the following week. Then I took a huge leap of faith and asked Lauren if she would like to go to a movie or catch up in town sometime soon. She took my request in her stride, unsurprised, and said she'd let me know by text if she could make it. We exchanged mobile phone numbers, and that was enough for me. Feeling like we'd come to the natural end of our conversation, I told her I'd go and see where the boys were, and she returned to her friends.

This was enough to keep my spirits high and I was hoping we could meet again soon. I told Matt our chat had gone well, and then had a couple of drinks, no longer so concerned about the effects of the alcohol.

I left the gathering that night buoyed by the possibility of spending more time with Lauren and getting to know her, and possibly even being lucky enough to be her boyfriend. While I thought about Lauren constantly, I was also focussed on my upcoming operations at the RCH to straighten my feet and align my hips. This was going to be my first major surgery for several years and I was anxious about both the operations and the recovery phase, which would put me back in a wheelchair for a long stint. This was annoying as I'd just started to go out with my mates, and met Lauren, and I saw the surgery as a major interruption to my social life. I couldn't see myself turning up to another party like the one I'd just been to in a wheelchair. But, as I always did, I agreed to the surgery as my doctors said it was what was best for me and would ultimately improve my walking.

It was the morning of my surgery; Mum and I had a six AM start and we were on the familiar road to the RCH by six thirty. I was still feeling nervous about the operation, but Mum had a way of making things feel right. "Just think how much better you'll be able to walk, run and kick the footy. Everything will work out for the best,

Hayden." Mum was always right, but on this occasion neither of us knew that a message I was about to receive from Lauren would turn my recovery upside down.

Sitting in the front seat of the car, my phone 'pinged' and Lauren's name appeared on my screen. I opened the message: "Hi Hayden, it was lovely meeting you on Saturday night. Thanks for asking me on a date, but I think I'd just like us to be friends. Good luck with your surgery. Lauren." I sat silently, staring out of the window, tears falling down my cheeks. The rejection was devastating.

I said nothing to Mum, I just sat there thinking to myself, 'Not again, not Lauren'. I thought Lauren was different. I thought she was going to give me a go.

When we arrived at the hospital, I met the clinical photographer who was assigned to take images of my feet before the surgery that Professor Kerr would no doubt use as a type of show-and-tell for other patients ahead of similar operations. Then, as soon the photographer was finished, I disappeared. I hid in the hospital playground, sitting on a chair in the outdoor basketball court, not wanting to see or speak with anybody. I kept looking at Lauren's message on my phone in despair, as Mum and Professor Kerr frantically searched for me, angry I'd missed my scheduled surgery time.

A male nurse who I'd met during previous hospital visits eventually found me sobbing in the playground. I told him about the bad news I had received, and he comforted me by assuring me there were 'plenty of fish in the sea' and that I should focus on the surgery and being able to improve my walking, which would also help me in meeting other girls later anyway. I agreed to go back with him into the hospital but not before making him promise to keep my secret, especially from my Mum and Professor Kerr.

When I returned, feeling guilty and ashamed, I made up a lie, telling them that I had run away because I didn't want to have the surgery, and that I felt I was walking well enough and didn't want to have to go through months of excruciating rehabilitation and physiotherapy.

With an understanding nod and gentle smile, Professor Kerr arranged for the nurses to prepare me for the op, which meant being naked, except for the white gown that tied up at the back in two places, and I was pushed on a trolley into the small room where the anaesthetist inserted a tube into my arm before asking me to count backwards from ten.

The general anaesthetic was a welcome relief, shutting down my consciousness, blocking out my emotional pain and giving me a temporary reprieve from the rejection I was suffering.

My surgery involved three procedures, the first being the releasing of my adductor muscles between my hips and my upper leg bones, the femurs. This was to enable more flexibility, and ultimately improve my ability to move.

Secondly, screws and plates were removed from my femurs that had been implanted during my previous hip operation. Every twelve months since my major hip surgery in primary school I had to undergo surgical modifications, a bit like taking my hips in for their annual service.

Finally, the bones in my big toes were fused together at the joints to relieve pain in the front of my foot. My big toes had been encroaching on my other toes, crushing them, and the surgery was designed to take pressure off my other toes and relieve the pain. The surgeries took several hours, and by 5 PM I was in the recovery room. Physically, I would recover well, however, emotionally I was at the beginning of another long journey, one that would make 2007 one of the most challenging periods of my life.

Recovering on the children's ward, my behaviour took a drastic turn, and it is something I can only explain by suggesting that perhaps it was triggered by the acute sense of rejection I felt from Lauren. At the tender age of just seventeen, I questioned whether my life was worth living.

According to my medical files, the nurses who were caring for me explained my behaviour as being confused, and stated that I had *'fears I had been part of a scientific experiment'*.

Two days after surgery I started throwing things across the room and, when questioned about my behaviour, simply told staff I was frustrated but wouldn't explain why.

Then, very late that same evening, I became verbally abusive toward the nurses, then became violent, furiously banging my fists on the bed and hitting the walls and even the staff. This out-of-character behaviour continued, with me reportedly talking very loudly and yelling, "*Kicking a goal for Kyneton!*" and, "*I'm not stupid!*". I talked about how I could see snow and rain in my room, and I nattered away to myself continuously.

It was as if I was away with the fairies. In my mind I believed that hospital staff were really girls from my school, dressed up as nurses.

I was anxious and would cry in my bed until the daily doses of diazepam calmed me down. This particular drug had a big impact on my state of mind, making me sing songs, laugh hysterically then yell out very loudly. I was only able to hold concentration for short periods of time and then I would become nonsensical.

My parents visited me in hospital but couldn't understand my behaviour; they were embarrassed and ashamed of me and my Dad didn't speak to me for an entire month and a half. My relationship with them suffered and would take a long time to return to normal.

I was moved to the adolescent ward as it was agreed that my behaviour could be better managed there, and that the environment would generally be more appropriate for me, considering I was a teenager. Once there, and after having ridden this bizarre rollercoaster of emotions for several days, I finally decided that I needed to confide in somebody about how I was feeling about everything.

A young male university student had been working on the ward and I thought he might understand. He was like a big brother-figure to me, he listened intently to my experience with Lauren, as well as the other girls, and then he talked me into having my doctors organise a consultation with the hospital's psychiatrist.

Feeling exhausted and hopeless, I agreed.

So, what should have been a seven-night hospital stay extended to more than two weeks at the RCH, as the specialists trialled drug after drug to help keep me balanced. Or, as the medical records state, *'settled and appropriate'*!

According to my medical records, at first it was thought that I had developed an acute psychosis, and a subsequent diagnosis of bipolar disorder, a condition associated with episodes of mood swings ranging from depressive lows to manic highs. My mental health diagnosis resulted in me starting treatment on the antipsychotic drug olanzapine, but it would be months before the correct dosage was determined and my wild swinging moods could be kept under control.

I was eventually discharged from the RCH but once at home I refused to believe there was anything wrong with me mentally and didn't take the prescribed medication. I was stubborn and couldn't understand why I needed to take drugs so I didn't. But within a week of returning to Kyneton I'd smashed Mum's Seven Dwarves Garden ornaments that lined our driveway. In a rage I picked each one up and threw them on the ground. My devastated parents didn't know how to handle my behaviour and I lashed out, punching Dad on the front lawn. He pinned me down and held me while I struggled to break free. My distraught Mum called the police who arrived quickly, handcuffing me and continuing to hold me down on our front garden until an ambulance arrived. It was a huge commotion in our street as I was forcibly put in the back of the ambulance and taken to the Anne Bayne Psychiatric Centre in Bendigo. I spent a full month there with other mental health patients, some of whom were undergoing drug rehabilitation programs, and many chose to walk around naked in the shared bathroom. I felt alone, uncomfortable, and out of place in these unfamiliar surroundings, they were very dark days.

I sat through dozens of counselling sessions as therapists tried to get to the bottom of why my rejection from Lauren had triggered my bipolar disorder, a diagnosis that was confirmed at the Bendigo Psychiatric Centre.

When I was finally allowed to go home my behaviour began to deteriorate again, and again I refused to acknowledge my bipolar and I stopped taking my medication again. The same cycle was repeated, my violent outbursts resulted in my parents calling the police, an ambulance followed, then my admission to the psychiatric centre. On one occasion I was so violent I was put in a padded cell for the safety of both myself and everyone else around me.

Following four separate admissions and four months as a resident at the psychiatric centre, my medication levels were adjusted, I began to accept that taking the drugs was in my best interest and my mood swings became less frequent and less violent. But the medication still had negative side-effects, causing big weight gains where I put on fourteen kilograms over a few months. I could no longer manage walking with my sticks and was forced to resort to using my electric scooter all the time. It's crazy to think that my mental health deterioration at seventeen began over a broken heart, but that's exactly what happened. I wish now I had never got in touch with Lauren on *Myspace*, and that horrible time in my life never happened. But now I accept that Lauren wasn't to blame. She had her reasons for not wanting to go on a date with me. She tried to let me down gently and continue a friendship with me. She couldn't know that her trying to be kind would trigger the unexpected and extreme reaction that plunged me into a deep and dark place.

With several months left of 2007, I had to think again about returning to school. I was in year ten and felt anxious about other students knowing about my recent mental health issues and admissions into the psychiatric ward. But I found the strength to go back to school, only to be confronted by rumours about me and Lauren having had an online relationship. Some schoolyard bullies, the weak-minded idiots who didn't usually need much incentive, started teasing me, shouting, "Why would such a popular girl like Lauren be interested in you? You're not going to get anywhere in life except for ending up in an institution!".

Their thoughtless, insidious comments hurt deeply, particularly after what I'd just experienced over those last few months. I hated school and wanted to leave, and I believed that was the only way forward. So, instead of going back to school again, I kept Dad company for a few weeks, sitting next to him while he drove trucks and delivered concrete to worksites across country Victoria. Thankfully our relationship had returned to the way it was before my mental health diagnosis, Dad and I were mates again, and it was wonderful spending time with him. Naturally, Sacred Heart wanted to know why I hadn't returned to school, so I agreed to meet with the principal and vice principal about my reasons for staying away.

With my parents by my side, I explained that I was embarrassed about my friendship with Lauren, and also about the bullying that I had endured once everyone found out about it. During this conversation, I explained that I didn't want to return to Sacred Heart again and that I would prefer to find a job and earn some money. But that wasn't to be. With the support of some good mates and teachers, I was convinced to see out my year ten studies as well as returning in 2008 to complete year eleven. The bullies were silenced, I was told the Principal had addressed them at an assembly, and as a result I managed to get through the few weeks left of the school year.

What a year that was! Just like the Queen's annus horribilis, 2007 was one that I would like to forget.

Chapter Eight

It was during year 11 at Sacred Heart that I got my first part-time job at a local supermarket.

Kyneton had been a two-supermarket town since the arrival of IGA in 2005, but Woolworths was much larger and was also one of the biggest employers in the town, after the local abattoir.

The careers advisor at school encouraged me to approach Woolworths to try to secure two weeks of work experience, a compulsory part of the Sacred Heart year eleven curriculum.

Despite feeling very nervous, after school one sunny afternoon I bravely rode my tricycle the few streets that led the way to my potential job at Woolies.

Arriving completely unannounced, the assistant store manager on duty, Simon Edwards, agreed to have a chat which I would later learn was very unusual, almost unheard of in fact, for an applicant with a disability to apply for a job in person at Woolworths. In most cases the parents or carer would apply on their behalf. Simon was impressed by my forthrightness, determination and confidence to make enquiries on my own and he agreed to let me start packing shelves for five dollars a day. I was absolutely over the moon and rode home excited about soon being able to join the workforce. Part-time jobs were very common for teenagers my age, and I wasn't going to be left behind. *"If they could do it, so could I"*, I thought to myself as I pedalled home, happy with my latest achievement.

A couple of days into the job, at the end of a long, seven-hour day packing shelves, Simon announced that all staff were to 'swarm' the store. I had no idea what swarming meant, apart from the thing that bees do. But I soon learnt that it involved all staff going down each aisle and turning the products around to ensure that all the labels faced the front. So, instead of going home after my shift had finished, I agreed to continue on with everybody else and join the swarm!

Being on my feet all day had been physically tiring, but mentally I wanted to keep going as I was still trying to impress the managers. Simon recognised that I was tired and told me it was up to me to pull the pin when I'd had enough. I was in the pasta sauce aisle and had started turning all the bottled sauces around, then moved onto the canned tomatoes. By the time I got to the tomato pastes I could barely keep my eyes open. But I was determined to keep going and rested my head on the shelf to keep me upright while I continued to turn the products around.

I was unaware at the time, but Simon had spotted me balancing unsteadily on my tired legs, holding both my sticks and my head on the tomato paste shelf. He must have been very impressed because he gave me a permanent part-time job that evening and I've now been working at Kyneton Woolworths for 13 years.

Simon told me years later that he'd said to a colleague that night as he held a jar of tomato paste, 'You know what, this company should forget bottling tomato paste and instead bottle Hayden's enthusiasm to work. Now that would be a best seller!' Securing my employment at Woolworths uplifted my spirits and gave me great joy, earning some money, feeling valued and having a purpose.

However, behind the scenes Simon had to work very hard to make it happen. Senior Woolworths executives had insisted I would only be employed if there was something in it for the business, like a government grant or subsidy. I thought it was sad that the heads of the organisation assumed my disability meant I would be less productive than other workers and therefore the business should be compensated financially for taking me on. I believe people with disabilities should have the same opportunities as people without disabilities, and businesses shouldn't have to be paid off for giving us employment. I proved that I wasn't a burden to my workplace at Woolworths, and I think that, without blowing my own trumpet, this is reflected in a reference Simon wrote for me:

"*Hayden proved to be, and still is, one of the most popular checkout operators at Kyneton Woolworths, with long queues at his register consistently. Once customers get to know Hayden, they work out days he is rostered and do their shopping on those days. On numerous occasions Hayden has received the 'Employee of the Week' award, and the number of items he puts through the register per minute is always up there with the best operators. Hayden is regularly mentioned in the Voice of the Customer survey, and the comments about him are always complimentary.*"

Simon Edwards

From the very early days at Woolworths, Simon fought for me to be employed because of the work ethic he witnessed in the pasta sauce aisle during the swarm. He also found a way to combat Woolworth's reluctance to employ me, by pulling out the "he'll be good for business" card. Woolworths had recently ended its meat contract with the local abattoir, *Hardwicks Meats*, resulting in around 100 townsfolk losing their jobs. It was a big hit to the town and forced unemployment levels up significantly. The supermarket's reputation was shattered, and when it opened up its new inhouse meat department protestors carried placards opposing the decision at the entrance of the store and eggs were thrown at the store windows. Simon argued with store management that employing me would be a good move and would help to get locals back onside. He hoped employing me would be an integral part of kick-starting a rebuild of Kyneton Woolworth's bad reputation.

Simon was determined to find a way to employ me and together with his wife Donna who was the store's customer service manager, they discovered a loophole in Woolworth's recruiting system. I was put through as a 'walk up' and didn't need any vetting by those at the executive level. Most Woolworth's employees applied online for their jobs, but Dad had always said to me, "If you want a job, you need to go and ask for it." So, thanks to Dad who suggested the 'walk up', and a mate of mine, Joel Bertoncini, who worked at Woolworths and put in a good word for me, I landed the job I was seeking.

As Simon put it, *"we slipped him through the cracks and employed him through the back door, and we have never looked back"*.

I am passionate about my job at Woolworths and I love my customers, particularly the elderly ladies and gentlemen who are often lonely and come to my register for a chat. I put a smile on their faces and that makes me feel good, too. We chat about things like what they're having for dinner and what their pets' names are, and they ask me how I'm going. Once, a generous customer anonymously gave $50 in an envelope to the customer service manager, with instructions written on it that it was a gift for me for being friendly and welcoming to customers. Another regular, who is a former Victorian Premier, once told me that I give great customer service and make people feel wonderful and welcome, which encourages them to come back and shop at Woolworths.

Unfortunately, however, not everyone is as friendly as he was. Some people abuse me and tell me I'm too slow putting their items through the register. Thankfully, and to the credit of my work colleagues, all of the other cashiers have my back and will assertively step in if they think I'm in any danger, or being treated unfairly. Simon is no longer working in management but still works in the store, and I know he keeps an eye on me during my shifts.

So, as a teenager with my first paid job, earning money at Woolworths meant I could start saving up for a car, which would be my next step toward independence.

It was during the same year I started working here that I applied for a training program at VicRoads. My Dad had worked as a cement truck driver and I had often travelled with him to projects in the Bendigo region. I loved watching the developing road projects unfold, and one of the biggest was a large roundabout being built on the Gisborne exit of the Calder Highway, south of Kyneton. I had a keen interest in VicRoads and working for the road authority became my career aspiration.

This dream came true much quicker than I could have imagined. My application to become a trainee was successful and I was excited to be able to start work in 2009. For me, that letter at the end of 2008 was the best Christmas present I could have received. It meant that I could leave school at the end of year 11 and begin a career I was truly excited about. It gave me a ticket out of school and the bullying that marred some of my time at Sacred Heart, where I hold so many great memories.

The VicRoads traineeship was based in Bendigo twice a week and in Kyneton once a week. I travelled by train to Bendigo where I began working in the registration and licencing department and in customer service, while I continued my part-time Woolworths job with two shifts a week. At VicRoads I processed applications for new drivers going for their L's and P's and took their photo that would appear on their new licence once they had passed.

Media alert! My employment at VicRoads was reported in the Shepparton News newspaper!

"Although Hayden Walsh has significant mobility issues and suffers from cerebral palsy, this has not prevented him from working in his dream job at VicRoads.

Worktrainers Castlemaine employment consultant Mark Sayer-Castle liaised with VicRoads who were supportive of workplace modifications funded through the Federal Government that allowed Hayden to complete all office-based tasks.

Modifications such as enlarged workspace to accommodate an electric scooter, installation of a saddle seat chair to increase stability, modified electronic cash drawer for easier access, computer and keyboard gel pads and electric stapler have all helped Hayden work more comfortably and productively.

Hayden is nearly halfway through an 18-month Business Administration Traineeship with VicRoads, working two days a week in Bendigo and one day a week in Kyneton. Now a valued member of the team, Hayden's confidence and independence has increased, and he happily uses public transport to travel to and from work.

Hayden remains in regular contact with Mark as part of the Worktrainers Post Placement Support Program and is grateful to him for helping find his dream job."

During my second year with VicRoads, I was nominated for the Customer Service Trainee of the year.

I couldn't believe that I was invited to their gala dinner awards night, as I'd been shortlisted for the state-wide honour. Not wanting to arrive unprepared, I did write a short speech, which I kept it in my pocket just in case I won. Mum and Dad were with me that night and I still remember the pride in their eyes when they called out my name as the winner of the 2010 VicRoads Customer Service Trainee of the Year. I was asked to go up to the podium to receive my trophy, a card and some cash, but I didn't have to make a speech, so my notes stayed in my pocket, which wasn't such a bad result, as by the time I made it up the steps to the podium I was out of breath and just happy to receive my award.

Many of the young people who came in to sit for their L's and P's were around my age, which depressed me as I wanted to get my licence, too. I wanted the same independence that all those other young men and women were able to experience once they got into their cars. I'd driven the electric scooter at secondary school, but the only other people I ever saw on them were older people with mobility issues. I was a young man and wanted a proper set of wheels too!

But some people, including my doctor, had reservations about my getting behind the wheel and they

If I can, you can

thought I would be a risk to other drivers on the road. I was determined to prove them wrong, and couldn't see why my CP should stop me from driving.

As you would guess by now, I wasn't going to sit back and let this latest challenge get the better of me! My parents supported my desire to get my learners permit, and Dad got me to study the rules booklet before sitting the test. I failed my learners' test three times before finally succeeding and being allowed to drive my Dad's car, proudly displaying L-plates on the front and back windows.

Dad began taking me for lessons in his white Commodore which proved too big for me to drive as my legs could barely reach the pedals, and the dashboard was too high. Instead, Grandma, whose driving days had coincidentally just come to an end, happily let me use her smaller Corolla to learn to drive in.

I also took some lessons in a smaller car provided by the driving school and the only modification I needed was to have a small knob attached to the steering wheel. An occupational therapist from Castlemaine sourced the knob, which I could grip hold of easily, as my crooked fingers were unable to be spread around a conventional steering wheel.

Like most other things I've really wanted, I was determined to achieve this next big milestone and in 2011, I successfully became another young adult legally allowed to drive without supervision!

After having worked two jobs for a few years I had saved enough money to buy my first car, a blue Corolla, that cost me twenty-eight thousand dollars. Mum and Dad told me they wouldn't be paying for a car as they expected me to pay my own way and earn my own money, so I was very proud of myself when I had finally accumulated the funds I needed for my first set of wheels.

I was able to drive myself to work, visit friends and get to the footy club to watch the mighty Kyneton Tigers, no longer having to rely on Dad to drive me everywhere. However, for the first six months a restriction was placed on my licence stating that I could only drive within a ten-kilometre radius of my home. Passing another driving test six months later would allow the restriction on my licence to be lifted, which I happily succeeded in, giving me even greater freedom and independence.

Turning twenty-one was one of my most memorable birthdays thanks to my godmother, Marcia, who, knowing how much I loved Nathan Buckley, gave me and my parents tickets to a Collingwood Football Club breakfast at the Holden Centre, Collingwood's home ground and location of their social rooms at the time.

About twenty diehard Collingwood supporters had been given the privilege of being welcomed into the inner sanctum to hear Nathan, who was assistant coach at the time, address his players. There were around 30 tables and at least one footy player sat on each table. We had Lachie Keeffe on our table, a Collingwood defender who later joined the Greater Western Sydney Giants.

I had met up with Nathan four years earlier at a Williamstown VFL game where he was coming back from a nasty hamstring injury and playing with Collingwood's

VFL affiliate team, the Williamstown Football Club. At half-time during this game against archrival Port Melbourne, the players were in their huddle before they left the field to head into the change rooms for the break. I managed to make my way up to Nathan and tapped him on the shoulder to say hello. I showed him a photo of the two of us I was holding, reminding him of his visit to the RCH 12 years earlier which seemed to trigger his memory, and he happily stopped to talk and have another photo taken with me.

At the Collingwood breakfast Nathan was equally as friendly again. He treated me like an old friend which made me feel very happy, particularly as it was my birthday. He said he couldn't forget my face and referred to me as 'Legend'. This was the third time I had met my idol, and it was overwhelming to have him give me his complete attention. Everybody had their eyes on Nathan—he was a club favourite—and he had chosen to chat with me. What a birthday present it was! Nathan was so very generous with his time and we talked about my work, the Kyneton footy club and how he had enjoyed his first year as assistant coach under Mick Malthouse. Another Collingwood player I really admired was Jarryd Blair. He was a young player from Wonthaggi, Victoria, when Collingwood gave him an opportunity as an 18-year-old. Jarryd also spent time talking to me and then invited me to meet some of his teammates, slowly walking with me around the room as I tottered on my sticks, introducing me to the other Collingwood players.

Many of the breakfast guests were people living with disabilities, which was no surprise because Collingwood has been very supportive of the disability community ever since I can remember.

If I can, you can

Then club president, Eddie Maguire, (or 'Eddie Everywhere' as he was commonly known due to his numerous high-profile media appearances each week) was at the breakfast that morning too. I'd met him at a previous Collingwood training session and when we met again that morning, he shook my hand like an old friend and wished me a happy birthday, too.

I loved the Collingwood Football Club so much that I desperately tried to find out how to get a job there. I trawled the club's website and discovered there were jobs being advertised in merchandising and also for being a water runner at training sessions and on game days. So, through my job agency, I applied for the roles, hoping that I could one day land my other dream job, having something to do with AFL footy and working for Collingwood. Unfortunately, I was never successful with my applications which was devastating as I had developed good customer service skills and I had a good football brain to boot! Maybe if they had me on-board, I could have been their lucky charm and they could have pulled off a win in the first 2010 grand final against St Kilda, instead of having to replay the match because of the draw.

News on the job front wasn't great in my 21st year, and by late 2011 my time at VicRoads came to an end. The Liberal state government at the time had a clean out of the public service, a cost-cutting measure, slashing money for the disability sector that had been used to include people with disabilities in the workforce. I was angry and upset about losing my job with VicRoads, it felt like the world was crashing down, not just for me but for others who also lost their jobs for the same reason.

Because of a change of management at Woolworths, I had to reapply for my job, but thankfully they kept me on and I spent the next fifteen months working on the checkouts, which I was very grateful for. It wasn't until 2012 that I secured some work experience at Western Water in Sunbury while I continued working at Woolworths. For the first six months I was unable to drive the 50 kilometres to get there because of the 10-kilometre licence restriction, so I caught the train to begin work at 9.30 every morning, then caught the train home each afternoon.

I worked in a range of areas at Western Water, including recycled water, archiving and customer service and I must have impressed somebody because soon after that job finished, I picked up a two-and-a-half-year contract at Central Highlands Water in Ballarat. In this new role I also worked in the customer service and community divisions, helping with administration and was involved with the organisation of community events like the Begonia Festival and school programs where I handed out recycled water bottles at local schools and at the North Ballarat Roosters Football Club, which was sponsored by Central Highlands Water. It seemed I was destined to be a water boy, maybe it had something to do with my love of the beach. Whatever it was that drew me to these organisations, they gave me a great sense of achievement and self-worth being part of a team, a workforce, doing positive things for the community.

It was during this time that I met a man called Gerard Dooley who was the Water Treatment Manager. He was older than me, probably the same age as my Dad, and over what always felt like the shortest hour of the day, the lunch break, we gradually struck up a friendship in the lunchroom, despite Gerard barracking for the Carlton Blues, the archrival of my beloved Collingwood Pies. Both of our teams had a pretty bad year in 2014 with Collingwood finishing eleventh on the AFL ladder and Carlton ending their season in thirteenth position. We spoke on many levels and covered many topics, including my career ambitions. I explained that had I not been offered the VicRoads traineeship at the end of year eleven, I would have liked to have gone on to study some sort of engineering or major projects degree. All of those early trips with my Dad in the concrete truck, watching major road and infrastructure projects unfold, had sparked an interest that I had retained.

Gerard felt that I was underutilised in my role in customer service as he believed that I could do much more than just putting letters in envelopes or handing out water bottles.

Gerard took it upon himself to arrange for me to be included on his journeys across country Victoria to various locations where he attended and assessed water treatment plants. On these trips I got to see parts of Victoria I'd never seen before, with varying landscapes and the many country towns, and we'd rate each town according to how good their vanilla slices were at their bakeries. It was like being on one big road trip with a mate, and I was also able to learn how different water plants functioned and how they serviced their surrounding towns. During our travels we would chat for hours about life, religion and work. But most of all, footy.

Soon after starting work with Central Highlands Water the condition on my driver's licence was lifted and I was then able to drive the seventy-one kilometres to Ballarat three days a week. It was a great relief to be able to drive, which took just over an hour, as the train journey on public transport had taken nearly three hours, just one way!

As much as it had been drilled into me about how dangerous night driving could be on country roads, nothing could have quite prepared me for what happened one night as I was driving home from Ballarat.

It was just starting to get dark and just as I took a bend following a straight stretch of road, a large grey kangaroo jumped out in front of me, colliding head-on with my Corolla. It happened so suddenly and gave me no time to react, and I doubt any driver would have been able to avoid the large animal. Shocked and shaking, I pulled over to the gravel on the side of the road. It was a deserted country road with no houses or streetlights in sight, just paddocks and farm fences that the kangaroo must have leapt over to make it onto the road I'd been traveling on.

As I sat in the car, I could see the lifeless kangaroo on the side of the road as another car that had been traveling in the opposite direction pulled over. Stunned and still shaking after this frightening ordeal, the female driver approached my car and, to my surprise, didn't bother asking how I was, and instead only asked me whether the kangaroo was still alive. Maybe she had expected me to be attending to the kangaroo instead of sitting in my car? The damage to my car was substantial, but could have been much worse. Swerving to avoid kangaroos on country roads accounts for many fatalities every year in Australia, when cars usually veer off the road and drive straight into tree trunks, other cars or down ditches. I was just grateful I escaped uninjured, but my car wasn't so lucky. Dad came and picked me up and organised a tow truck to collect my car.

In early 2015 the AFL wanted to promote more rural community engagement and one of the games of the preseason competition, the NAB Cup, was Carlton vs. Collingwood at the Queen Elizabeth Oval in Bendigo, at 4.10pm on a Friday. Gerard offered to pick me up from my place, then the two of us drove the fifty minutes up the Calder Freeway, excitedly teasing each other about whose team was going to win. As you would expect, this was a pretty big deal for a small regional city like Bendigo, so locals from all around turned out in huge numbers, alongside Pies and Blues fans who had made the two-hour journey north from Melbourne.

Before the game we ate lunch at the National Hotel, which was across the road from the QEO, then wandered over, ensuring we gave ourselves plenty of time to gain entry and find our seats before the match began. Once inside, we headed for the area set aside for people with disabilities which gave us a great view of the game from the forward pocket near the goals.

But before we got there, we were stopped by none other than my mate, Nathan Buckley, who was now the senior coach of the Pies, as well as club president, Eddie Maguire. They were both really happy to see me and each greeted me with a big bear hug. Gerard couldn't believe it! Two of the biggest names in the AFL, which was pretty much a religion in Victoria, both knowing me by name and welcoming me with open arms.

My friendship with Nathan had been reignited at the Collingwood breakfast a few years earlier and since then I'd been attending the club's annual best and fairest vote count, the Copeland Trophy. It was a huge honour to be offered a ticket to attend the night, which was usually just for players, their partners, club officials and a limited number of members. But as I mentioned, the Collingwood

Football Club's community spirit was one of its strengths, and this extended to their biggest night of the year when Jarryd Blair invited me to the function, knowing how much it would mean to me to be on his table.

The first Copeland Trophy I attended was in 2013 at the Palladium at Crown Casino, one of Melbourne's most prestigious event venues. Making sure I looked the part, I dressed up in a black suit and topped it off with my black and white Collingwood tie which Mum helped fold into a neat Windsor knot. My parents took the opportunity to have a night out, too, and offered to drive me to the Best and Fairest event.

Once there, Mum and Dad accompanied me in the lift to the first floor where the function was being held in a dining room that could fit over one thousand guests. My parents left me on my own and went for dinner at one of the restaurants on the ground level before going their separate ways, Mum to play the pokies, and Dad to have a beer and watch some cricket in the sports bar.

I stood in the foyer feeling awkward and shy, surrounded by a sea of colourful, shiny frocks worn by women sipping champagne with their smartly suited up partners. I wondered to myself how a bogan from a small country town like Kyneton got to mix it with famous city slickers. Then I made a beeline for the dining room, I bypassed the drinks waiters and headed inside the enormous venue, wanting to find my table before proceedings began. What I didn't want was to be the last person limping into the room with my sticks when everybody else was seated. I wished I had a partner in a beautiful shiny frock that could walk with me and sit with me, but I had no reason for concern, as Jarryd spotted me through the crowd, and took me to my seat before ordering me a beer to settle my nerves.

That night Scott Pendlebury, one of the club's best players and another of my faves, won his second best and fairest trophy and went on to captain the club the following year. It was also on this night that I had another photo taken with Nathan which I still use as my profile picture on my *LinkedIn* account. Surely there's no harm in promoting to prospective employers who my celebrity mates are! It was a night to remember, almost like a fairy tale, with me surrounded by my idol and favourite players, being served up a three-course meal and having my drinks poured for me.

I kept up my connections with Jarryd Blair and Jordan De Goey, who sometimes texted me to see if I'd like to watch their training sessions. On one occasion someone pulled a few strings which ended up with me being asked to go onto the training oval and have a kick with Nathan and Jordan. As usual, the television news cameras were there in the hopes that they would 'get a scoop' with any injury worries or controversies to report ahead of the weekend games. But this time (it must have been a slow news day!) they instead filmed me having a kick with the lads, which, once again, had me in the spotlight on the news that night. What the media didn't know was that after the morning kick with the boys, Nathan invited me to join the team for lunch. Now that would have been a scoop! In fact anything to do with AFL, particularly in my home state of Victoria is usually newsworthy

So, there we were, standing at Bendigo's Queen Elizabeth Oval with Eddie and Nathan, who, after a few minutes of us catching up, had to head into the change rooms to get their players revved up for the match. Gerard, who still couldn't quite believe who he had been talking to, wished them luck for the game and we continued on to our assigned seats.

As we got closer, I spotted a young guy, about 15 years old in a Carlton guernsey, sitting in our seats. I politely told him he shouldn't be there because it was reserved for people with disabilities, but to my shock and embarrassment, he explained that he had CP and was entitled to be there also. I quickly apologised and we ended up getting on well, we had lots in common and spent a great afternoon together. I learnt that he had a milder version of cerebral palsy than I did, he didn't need any mobility assistance and his speech was very good. I felt bad that I had jumped to conclusions about this Carlton supporter, who had done nothing wrong. I wondered maybe if he'd been wearing a Collingwood jumper, I wouldn't have said anything?

I had never seen so many people at the QEO in my whole life. This oval was the home ground for South Bendigo, one of the ten teams which made up the Bendigo Football Netball League. Nine and a half thousand spectators packed the grandstand, which was almost at full capacity, while South Bendigo's social club rooms were bursting at the seams, everyone eager to eye a piece of the action. The only other times I'd been to the QEO had been to watch the mighty Kyneton Tigers, when crowds were considerably thinner, usually just a few hundred.

The match was a low-scoring one and to the delight of Gerard and our new Blues-loving friend, Carlton won by 7 points.

Another time Gerard and I attended an AFL game together was when we went to the home of the Western Bulldogs to watch Collingwood play. I was usually very vocal at the footy and loved calling out to some of my favourite players in Dane Swan and Scott Pendlebury, "Go Swanny!", "Go Pendles!"

Sitting in front of us was a group of women barracking for the Western Bulldogs, so they were very confused when I started cheering for one of their players, yelling out, "Go Jack! Kick a goal, Jack!" I was actually barracking for Jack Redpath who played for the Bulldogs at the time, but only because I grew up with him in Kyneton and he was also one of my favourite players, even though he wasn't a Magpie. One of the women turned to me in a huff and asked, "Are you going for the Magpies or the Bulldogs?" By this stage they were bamboozled because everybody knows Collingwood supporters are one-eyed, it was unheard of for a Pies supporter to barrack for a player from an opposing team. They didn't turn around again, but I kept yelling out to Jack, hoping he might hear me in the crowd.

For most of my working life, I have been lucky enough to work two jobs at the same time, but this cannot be said of all people living with disabilities. Only about half the number of Australians between 15 and 64 who live with disability are employed. That means there are low participation rates and high unemployment within the disability population. Unfortunately, the statistics get worse in relation to discrimination with almost one in five workers with a disability aged between 15-24 experiencing discrimination, mostly by their employers.

The cost of living with a disability cannot be ignored, and I was grateful in 2013 for the financial entitlements that I began receiving through the Federal Government's National Disability Insurance Scheme (NDIS).

Expenses associated with my disability began around the time of my diagnosis at thirteen months, then the ongoing costs rolled around every year since then for lower leg splints and walking sticks. As a young boy I was a wheelchair user, our home needed modifications to accommodate me and there were ongoing trips to hospital with costs including petrol, parking, food and medications.

According to Australia's Cerebral Palsy Alliance, it costs an average of $43,431 to care for a person with cerebral palsy every year with the financial cost to the family or individual being around $16,000. The remaining costs are funded mainly through government and non-government organisations. My NDIS entitlements enabled funding for my splints and sticks, as well a social living allowance that enabled an NDIS carer to accompany me to AFL games so that I could watch the mighty Collingwood Magpies. NDIS payments also covered my weekly physiotherapy sessions with local physio and friend Patrick 'Patty' Rowe accompanying me to my swimming sessions, or NDIS worker Edward Higgs who went running with me at the Kyneton Showgrounds. The NDIS aimed to identify people with disabilities who had been falling through the cracks, so to speak, and give them the support and funding they needed to live better lives. Time would only tell whether the scheme would be successful.

Chapter Nine

I don't think I would have made it through my adolescent years if it hadn't been for sport. That might sound strange coming from a person living with a disability, but for me, sport became my emotional and physical lifeline.

After being forced out of playing Aussie rules football when I was thirteen, I lost my passion for the game for a long time. I didn't play or attend footy in my town or any of Collingwood's games. It was a four-year footy drought which, looking back, is hard to imagine now. However, luckily, I reconnected with football at the age of seventeen, when my new integration aide at Sacred Heart, Deb Thaw, reintroduced me back into the Kyneton Football Netball Club. Deb knew I'd been through a particularly tough few months and figured reigniting connections at the footy club was one way of getting me out of the house and back into the community. Deb was the wife of the KFNC President, Jeff Thaw, and she suggested I come down to the Kyneton Showgrounds to watch the Under 18's training session. Suffice to say, it didn't take long for me to fall back in love with game. The KFNC was a good family club and it was in desperate need of volunteers. Under 18's coaches Anthony 'Oakie' O'Connor and Mark 'Tunz' Tunzi welcomed me aboard and I started running water for the team, positioning myself in the forward pocket near the goal square. I'd stagger onto the ground with a drink bottle in each hand replacing my sticks and the players really appreciated that I could help to quench their thirst. It was an exhausting task, juggling two plastic containers, each filled with almost one litre of water, but I felt like I was part of the team. I got to celebrate with the mighty Tigers when they won by joining in the circle, arms across one another's shoulders and singing the song together loud and proud. And, if the team lost, I'd commiserate with them by slowly moving around the change rooms after the game and give each player a consoling pat on the back as they sat on the floor, usually with their head hanging between their knees. But win or lose, we always shared a beer together after the games in the social club rooms.

I spent a couple of years running water until I was bowled over on the oval a couple of times by players from opposition teams. Senior players are big men, usually in their twenties and sometimes over one hundred kilograms. Having one of them collide with me, even accidentally, was like being rammed by a raging calf that had escaped from its paddock. It was agreed I would be much safer managing the interchange box on the side of the oval where I recorded the players' numbers as they came on and off the bench during the games. But I didn't mind what role I played at the club, as long as I was involved.

Being a part of a community sports club has always given me opportunities to keep fit while training with other footy players. Becoming a volunteer has also enabled me to make friends and contribute in a positive way. It has given me a purpose and drive that is both rewarding and enjoyable. It's been fourteen years since I began in my first volunteering roles and I'm proud to say I still put in a few hours every week at the club and am proud of the contribution I make to the Kyneton Tiger's community, now as the senior men's timekeeper.

The football club played an important and consistent role following my most difficult teenage year, my annus horribilis, which brought about some of the greatest challenges I have faced in my life. I am grateful to have been able to bounce back after my mental health issues took their toll, and the football club was one of the places where I then felt most safe and valued.

My affiliation with the local footy club, as well as my reinvigorated support for my beloved Collingwood Magpies, triggered a desire in me to play footy again myself, and a random evening out paved the way for this to happen.

It was during 2014 when I was twenty-four and I went to a dinner dance at the Kyneton Bowling Club, which was organised by Windarring, a local community-based organisation that helps integrate people with disabilities into the community. The event was held during National Disability Week and had been advertised in the local papers. It was a fun night and me and my horse-riding friend, Morgan, with whom I'd kept in touch, hit the dance floor, me with my sticks and Morgan with her wheelchair. What a sight we were!

That night I got chatting to a photographer, Mitchell McCann, who was taking some publicity shots for the papers. He didn't live with a disability but worked in the disability sector in Bendigo. He mentioned to me that there was an all-abilities footy club based in Echuca and wondered if I would be interested in playing for them. While I desperately wanted to play footy for my hometown club, the KFNC had no all-ability teams, so, deciding I had nothing to lose (other than my sticks!) I got in touch with the Echuca coach who invited me to attend training.

Dad offered to drive me the hour and a half it would take to get from Kyneton to Echuca for training, worried that after a strenuous training session I would be too tired to drive myself home. He was right. Once I got into a training session, I gave it everything I had, determined to be the best footballer I could be. So much so that on the way home I usually fell asleep for most of the journey back to Kyneton! Twice a week we made the three-hour, round-trip to footy training, then on weekends our game could be in any of Echuca's surrounding country towns of Shepparton to Wodonga, often hundreds of kilometres away. If only there were frequent driver points for the number of kilometres we travelled every week! Dad sure put in a huge effort to support my sporting endeavours, which he knew were important for both my physical health and emotional wellbeing.

I spent the next couple of years playing for the Echuca/Moama Rockets in a team made up of players from the Victoria and New South Wales border towns and the surrounding districts. All players lived with either intellectual or physical disabilities, varying from cerebral palsy, Down syndrome, missing limbs to visual impairments and autism, just to name a few. It was the first time I had been on a team of players who were also disabled. We shared a love of football and being connected, but the most common link was our desire to be included, to be able to participate, not be relegated to being spectators. Ensuring people living with disabilities are included is such a powerful way of displaying an acceptance of us and showing that we are worthy and valued members of any community.

My contribution as a volunteer at the Kyneton Football Netball Club was documented during a television news report that veteran Channel Seven News reporter, Nick MacCallum, filmed at the Kyneton Showgrounds early in 2006. He was producing a series of stories for Channel Seven News about club legends and had heard that I'd been a volunteer at the KFNC for eight years and that I lived with a disability. Nick and his crew, a camera operator and sound assistant, came to training at the Kyneton footy club on a freezing Tuesday night, rugged up in their puffer jackets, beanies and gloves. It was around six PM and the Showground oval lights were barely visible through the fog that had already descended on the ground. The excitement of having the television crew there got my adrenalin flowing, warming me from the inside as the players all gave me high fives as they ran out onto the oval. This was captured by the camera crew and would be the opening shots for Nick's story. During my interview with Nick, the cameraman positioned me on the oval so that the team could be seen training in the background. He asked me about my reason for volunteering and what was so special about the club. I was so excited about being interviewed and took the opportunity to share my dreams and hopes, not only for me but for all people with disabilities.

To finish off the story, the crew filmed me running my usual lap at the end of the seniors' training session. It was a real struggle for me, I was freezing and my muscles were aching, but a couple of the players always slowed their pace down to mine, keeping me company and encouraging me to finish the lap.

The following Friday night, Mum, Dad and I sat on the couch at home, eager to watch Nick's story about me. We sat through most of the Channel Seven News bulletin and began to wonder whether it would ever come on! Thankfully, just before the weather, the spot in the news when an uplifting, feelgood story is told, presenter Peter Mitchell's face lit up as he read the introduction to my story, "*The most valuable player at the Kyneton Football Netball Club never actually makes it onto the ground during* matches. Hayden Walsh suffers from cerebral palsy but still takes part in every training session, inspiring his teammates with his courage and determination."

I was glued to the television and laughed out loud when I finally saw myself leaning up against the boundary fence as the players ran past me giving me high fives. The story only ran for about a minute and a half, but Nick squeezed in lots of shots of me encouraging the players during their drills with the footy, as well as a couple of snippets of me from our interview. Nick had asked me, "What motivates you to keep doing what you're doing?" to which I answered, "*A lot of people say I can't do stuff and I prove them wrong. I love proving people wrong.*" Then there were more pictures of me in the redbrick time-keepers' box where I spent my Saturday afternoons, followed by another snippet from me: "*I'd love to be out there if I didn't have cerebral palsy. My dream ever since I was little was to play AFL football.*"

There was some old footage Nick had found in the Channel 7 archives of me playing Auskick during that AFL game in 2001. Nick's voiceover said, "*He can't play matches, but he did once when he was 11 at half-time in an AFL game. He became a local hero when he spoiled an opponent's mark.*"

I'd actually forgotten how seriously I'd taken that game, and my parents were shocked at what I said next: "*He was going for the ball and I got my stick and then belted him*". We had a good laugh and watched the end of the story, which showed players Benny Weightman and Ryan Carrafa slowly jogging with me around the oval, before Nick signed off, "Nick MacCallum, Seven News".

The day after the story went to air, I was lucky enough to get another chance to play footy at half-time during an AFL match. This time I was playing with my all-abilities team, the Echuca Moama Rockets at Etihad Stadium, now known as Marvel Stadium.

One of the volunteers for the Rockets, Jason McCurrie gave me a hand in the change rooms lacing up my runners. I had managed to ditch the Blundstones that I had to resort to wearing as a child, but unfortunately, I was still unable to wear football boots, as no sporting footwear companies had come up with a design that could accommodate my AFO's. Wearing runners wasn't ideal on an often slippery and muddy surface, as it usually resulted in me slipping and sliding through a forward pocket and onto my backside or faceplanting, but I had no other choice. Hmm… maybe there's my opportunity to make my millions!

By this stage, I didn't use my sticks when I was on the playing oval, but in the event of my falling over, one of the trainers would run out onto the ground and give me my sticks to help me get myself up.

While our team was warming up in the changerooms, AFL teams North Melbourne and the Sydney Swans were battling it out late in their second quarter. I could hear the crowd roaring as one of the sides had kicked a goal just seconds before the siren sounded, signalling half time. That was our cue to head up the race and onto the ground for our exhibition game. But just as I approached the bright green turf the weirdest thing happened. Spectators in the grandstand near me started yelling out my name and cheering for me. "Hayden, you legend!" "Go Hayden!" "Go H!" was bellowed from the stands from several footy fans I had never seen before in my life. Then the penny dropped; some of the spectators at the game must have seen my story on Seven News the previous night. Maybe I was becoming a celebrity after all! I made my way out onto

Etihad's oval, excited footy fans had acknowledged me, bringing back memories of my Auskick days.

After the game, Jason McCurrie and I hung out together to watch the rest of the North versus Sydney match, then afterwards he sat and chatted with me while I waited to catch the Kyneton-bound train from Southern Cross station. By my mid-twenties I was comfortable travelling on public transport at night alone, and chose to leave my car at home as I was usually too tired to drive after a game. Jason was from the country but had moved to Melbourne to study sports management and suggested we head out on the town the next time I was there.

I started spending some weekends in Melbourne with Jason and his group of friends. It was my first real taste of freedom as I was still living at home with my parents. I would joke with Jason and tell him I was coming to Melbourne and we were going out to meet some women! We'd go to the footy or to the pub and have a few beers, or have dinner at different restaurants with his friends, who were kind to me and made me feel welcome as a newcomer to their group. Other times we'd go and enjoy live music at The Worker's Club in Fitzroy. On one occasion Jason and I got chatting to some women at the bar, but just when they excitedly started organising where we could go for the next round of drinks, I could feel myself running out of steam. It was around midnight and I felt like Cinderella at the ball when her carriage turned into a pumpkin because that's when I started to feel tired because of the bipolar medication I was taking. Jason called it a night and we went back to his house so I could get some sleep. "All talk, no action", Jason would say to me. But the women would have to wait, I needed my sleep!

Our friendship was deep, and Jason confided in me that he suffered from anxiety, which I had also experienced sporadically since my bipolar diagnosis. He told me of his Obsessive Compulsive Disorder and that he had a mild condition of Tourette Syndrome, a nervous system disorder involving repetitive, involuntary muscle movements or involuntary vocal sounds or words. He spoke freely about his conditions and I spoke openly about my cerebral palsy and the mental health issues I'd faced as a seventeen-year-old. We would pick each other up and suggest ways of getting on top of our demons. This usually involved a good laugh, exercising and a good feed.

After a long walk one sunny Saturday afternoon along the Brighton beachfront where, thankfully, there is a concrete boardwalk which saved me from getting bogged in the sand with my sticks, Jason and I had a kick of the footy then went for a coffee at a local café. Because of my regular visits to Brighton during summer holidays as a child, many of the café owners and locals around the shopping strip recognised me and would all say, "G'day, Hayden!" Jason couldn't believe it and joked, "Maybe I should call you Eddie Everywhere!"

Friendships are extremely important to me and I put a lot of effort and time into maintaining relationships. Whether it be a simple text asking how my mates are going, or a good old-fashioned phone call, I like to keep in touch. These are the people who I call upon if I need advice or mentoring, and I like to think they get a buzz out of hearing from me, too.

In 2018 when the Bendigo Dockers football club entered an all-abilities team into the league, I was quick to thank the Echuca/Moama Rockets for the opportunity to play with them, then change allegiances to the Dockers. This immediately halved my travel time to get to training in Bendigo twice a week from four hours to two hours, which made things much easier for me.

The Bendigo Dockers All-Abilities team, which was later renamed the Bendigo Suns, had three coaches all called Daniel. At my first training session one of the Daniels, Daniel Ridgeway, suggested to me that I should bring some of my mates to the next training session to see if they wanted to join the team too. Wondering why any of my able-bodied friends would want to play in our team, let alone even be allowed to, I replied, "But my mates don't have any disabilities!". Daniel assumed that because I had CP, my friends would be disabled, too. It was an innocent assumption, but one that was and still is a common belief among some people who don't live with disability. Daniel was embarrassed and has since told me that that was a lightbulb moment for him, a turning point. He never again assumed anything about people who live with disabilities, and I'm proud to say that I think he learnt a lot from me during our time together.

While I enjoyed playing football and loved being part of a team, I hadn't managed to kick a goal for Bendigo, and it was already midway through the season. There were plenty of other players who had more physical ability than I did, so as well as playing the game, my role had become one of encouraging my teammates before games. A few of the guys knew I really wanted to kick a goal and during a game on July 8th against my old team, the Echuca/Moama Rockets, they made it happen, feeding the ball to me near the goals, enabling me to dribble it through the goal posts. You would have thought we had won the grand final the way everyone carried on! Every single player on the ground, including my former teammates, got around me to celebrate my first goal for the season. It was an amazing feeling and one I still smile about now.

The Bendigo Suns won the premiership in its first year, and it was during that final that I kicked my second goal for the season, capping off a great year with the team. We celebrated at the Suns' clubrooms near Bendigo's Weeroona Lake where photos were taken of our team and we sang the club song loud and proud. A large crowd had turned out to watch the game, which was just one of a series of finals to be played that day. There was no alcohol allowed after the games, so we drank soft drinks and toasted our win with cans of Coke and Fanta.

As much as I loved football, it hadn't been my only sporting pursuit. When I was eighteen, I decided to step up my involvement in sporting activities and to see just how far I could push myself. I found out where the annual tryout days were being held for the various Paralympic squads and locked them into my calendar. Trial locations were set up at several Melbourne locations and anybody with a disability was welcomed to have a go. I chose swimming, soccer and athletics because they were sports that I thought I could excel in, particularly swimming as I'd had a lot of experience in the water with all of my trips to the beach and in the local pool during my years of physiotherapy sessions. I'd also loved tuning into the Olympics every four years and had been glued to the television during the 2000 Olympics that were hosted in Sydney.

As I was very independent, my parents no longer felt the need to accompany me on every outing so instead, one of my carers drove me to Melbourne and became my helper for the duration of the Paracamp tryout weekend. He helped check me into the Albert Park hotel and ensured I got to the pool, running track and soccer oval on time for every session.

The swimming trials were first on my list and I quickly discovered that while I wasn't a bad swimmer, I was finishing my heats at the back of the pack and was too slow. I was also a slow runner, but my efforts in some of the athletic field events earnt me an invitation to attend the Essendon Athletics Club for further trials. They invited me to compete in the discus and shotput competitions, but given the difficulty I had gripping the round, flat disc and heavy, metal shotput ball, I'd convinced myself there was no future for me in these events, long before I received a phone call confirming my suspicions.

However, on the upside, soccer came up trumps for me in the tryouts and I was invited to train with the Victorian Pararoos soccer team! Playing for the Pararoos provided one of the sporting highlights of my life when I was representing Victoria in the National Paralympic Championships against South Australia. We wore the Victorian blue and white colours, while the South Australian jersey was red and white. All of the players either lived with an acquired brain injury or cerebral palsy, so it was a fairly level playing field, and I was positioned in the forward line as a striker. Large crowds turned out to watch our game and I got a total of three kicks. The Victorians didn't win but it was a proud moment when our team was presented with bronze medals for coming third in the competition.

Sport has been such an important part of my life, for my emotional and physical health, as well as socially, and many of my strongest friendships began in or around sporting clubs.

When I was growing up, I had no sporting idols who lived with disability to look up to or consider as role models. Today there are so many amazing people with disabilities who are leading the way by showing the world that we are just like anybody else, with our own hopes and dreams.

Australian sportsman and 2022 Australian of the Year Dylan Alcott is doing some great work in this field. The phenomenal sportsman has won gold medals in wheelchair basketball, as well as becoming the first man in any form of tennis to earn the calendar year golden slam of all four major titles and the gold at the 2021 Tokyo

Paralympics. He's also done some pretty crazy stuff like crowd surfing at music festivals in his wheelchair!

I was lucky enough to meet Dylan at a business lunch in Bendigo in 2018 when I was working briefly at Coliban Water. I wasn't with the company for very long, but long enough to be invited onto a table of ten for a luncheon at Bendigo's All Seasons Resort Hotel where Dylan was the guest speaker. Wheeling his wheelchair up onto the podium, Dylan told us he was born with a tumour on his spinal cord that impacted his mobility, and that he had been a wheelchair user all his life. He proudly told us how his disability hadn't stopped him from achieving his own goals, and that his charity and business, the *Dylan Alcott Foundation* helped other young people living with disabilities to fulfil their potential by offering grants to children who show talent in their chosen field. I had my photo taken with Dylan that day and the smile on my face shows just how inspired I was by him.

That night I posted a photo of Dylan and myself from the luncheon on my Instagram and Facebook pages, proud to be rubbing shoulders with such a legend. My encounter with Dylan was a memorable one, and little did I know at the time that in just a few years, the Dylan Alcott Foundation would call upon me to help them!

I'm no sporting star, but I hope my sporting endeavours inspire some children or adults living with a disability to achieve their sporting dreams too. At the age of 28, I still hoped my dream of playing for the Kyneton Tigers would come to fruition one day, but as my grandfather would always say, 'good things come to those who wait'.

Chapter Ten

As a 28-year-old I had learnt so much about life and living, I'd experienced extreme highs and lows, as well as deep feelings of joy and sadness. I had lived a full life working and playing sport, I had good friends and family and my beautiful partner Yessah. I had lived with pain, medications, medical appointments, procedures, recoveries and rehabilitations. But nothing could have prepared me for what happened next.

On a March evening in 2019, I was enjoying dinner with Yessah, my beautiful partner of 13 months, in our small unit in Kyneton. Yessah was 39 weeks pregnant and our baby was due in just 2 days. A growing sense of anxiety had built as our baby's birth became imminent, and Yessah's stomach was so big it looked like it could have burst. Niggling pains deep in Yessah's belly throughout the afternoon were tell-tale signs that our unborn baby was preparing to enter the world.

We had packed Yessah's overnight bag to take to the hospital and it had been sitting near the front door for a couple of weeks, ready for an immediate exit. Our biggest concern was that Yessah would go into labour and deliver the baby quickly and at our apartment. I had no idea what I could do to help if that happened, so we were taking these initial pains seriously.

Yessah FaceTimed her mother in France, where it was late morning, for advice on when we should make the call and get Yessah to the hospital, but she urged us to sit tight, and for Yessah to have a shower to ease the pain. Very little of our evening meal was eaten that night and

Yessah told me to be ready to drive her to the hospital at any moment. I nervously paced up and down the short hallway between our bathroom and kitchen with my sticks clattering louder than usual on our wooden floorboards. All I could hear was Yessah moaning in pain in the shower. I felt sick with worry and called my mum who was also stressed out of her head. After a fifteen-minute shower, Yessah's pain had not subsided and she told me it was time to go. I was freaking out thinking about getting Yessah to the hospital, but told myself over and over that once she was there, she would be safe. It was a frantic few minutes as we bundled Yessah's bag into the car before I carefully helped her into the front seat, stretching the seatbelt to its limit around her huge belly, before buckling it in with my shaking hands. With my most precious cargo on board, I drove carefully through the backstreets of Kyneton, until the red and white neon 'Emergency' sign appeared, immediately easing my anxiety a little. My disability parking sticker enabled me to drive my car right up to the emergency entrance to the hospital where, as quickly as I could, I got out of the car, got my sticks from the back seat and staggered around the other side of the car to help Yessah out of the car.

A nurse approached us and went around to Yessah, helping her to waddle towards the main doors. At this point I wished she had brought a wheelchair for her, instead. In fact, I was trembling with worry and unsteady on my feet and could have done with one myself! She then ushered us into a private room in the hospital's urgent care department and began assessing Yessah's condition by taking her blood pressure, temperature and checking to see whether her waters had broken. I held Yessah's hand as a foetal heart monitor was strapped to her belly, then we heard our baby's magical heartbeat, an instant trigger that never failed to set off a torrent of Yessah's emotional tears. For me, the heartbeat was as comforting as a familiar beat from one of my favourite Pet Shop Boys' songs, reassuring me and enabling me to relax just a little. Knowing Yessah was in good hands and getting medical attention calmed me down. We had booked in for Yessah to deliver the baby at the Bendigo Hospital, an hour's drive from Kyneton, so when the nurses announced her cervix was dilated to 3 centimetres and her contractions were only 6 minutes apart, they declared it was time to call an ambulance and transfer Yessah to Bendigo to give birth there.

Knowing I would be a bundle of nerves, Dad arrived at the Kyneton Hospital to support us, and offered to drive me to the Bendigo hospital, while Yessah was taken by ambulance. She told me later that a wonderful male paramedic had kept her calm during the trip, spending the journey relaying the birthing stories of his own daughters, which all had happy endings.

Dad and I first drove to their house where I saw Mum briefly and she was still stressing about the impending birth, but was adamant she wasn't coming to Bendigo with us (Mum has never liked hospitals, they bring back bad memories) and instead asked that Dad keep her up to date with hourly phone calls. Dad was in total control as he drove me the 65 kilometres to the Bendigo Hospital, the entire time I was petrified Yessah would give birth in the back of the ambulance.

We were about half an hour out of Bendigo when my phone rang. It was Yessah letting me know that the ambulance had just arrived and that she was being taken to the birthing ward where I should go to upon my arrival.

Dad and I hotfooted it straight there after he parked the car as I was just desperate to get to Yessah's side and hold her hand. Thankfully, when we saw her sitting up in bed in a shared room with other expectant mothers, she seemed more comfortable as the pain relief she'd been given in the ambulance had achieved the desired effect.

But several hours later, around two AM, the doctors told us we should take Yessah back home until the baby was ready to be born—the dash to Bendigo had been a false alarm! This is when Mum, speaking by telephone from her home in Kyneton, stepped in. Just as she did at the Auskick match when officials sat me on the bench to watch the game, Mum told the nurse that under no circumstances was Yessah to be discharged and sent home before the baby was born. Mum, Dad and I were all very worried that if we went back to Kyneton the baby could be born at our apartment, or, even worse, in the back of the car during another trip along the Calder Freeway. After all, we were only a couple of days away from the baby's due date. Taking on my first fully fledged role as father to our unborn child, I told the doctor in charge that Yessah was to remain in the hospital until we were holding our first baby in our arms. And, I am very proud to say that I was victorious!

Yessah was admitted to a single room so Dad drove me back to their house where I could get some sleep, or at least try to, knowing that I could return soon enough to be by my partner's side.

When we arrived later that morning, we found Yessah comfortably sitting up in her bed happily telling us she had no pain and could feel no contractions. I was thrilled that I hadn't missed anything and that she was so comfortable. But then she explained that a couple of hours earlier the doctor had broken her waters, which brought on the contractions faster and more painful than the night before. She said she'd been given gas for pain relief which she breathed through a mask over her nose, but when that didn't help, she had begged the nurses for an epidural, describing her pain as being similar to having her insides squeezed, like a drenched towel is wrung out after being dragged out of a swimming pool. She had been granted her epidural which involved a large needle being pressed into a section of the spinal canal with magical fluid inserted that numbed Yessah's body from the waist down to her toes.

As I sat next to Yessah as she dozed off from the extreme lack of sleep, I felt that this was a peaceful time and that things were very calm, and I started to get really excited about the birth and meeting my new baby.

It was several hours before there were any signs of the baby arriving and during this time Dad and I went for walks outside the hospital, drank cups of tea and ate sandwiches at the hospital cafeteria. Then, by late afternoon, we were made aware of the first signs that the real action was about to start. Nurses informed us that the baby wasn't far away, and they began preparing Yessah for the birth while escorting me into the room so I could be present.

Stirrups were set up for her legs to be placed in at the end of the bed and a doctor checked to see if the baby's head was crowning. It was at this point that it all became a bit too much for me, I felt sick with worry, I began sweating profusely and felt like I might faint. An observant nurse noticed the colour drain from my face then slowly turn a sickly shade of green, and guided me from the birthing suite to a nearby waiting room with Dad.

With a sick bag in my hands, memories began flooding back about the warnings from doctors that there was a chance that my children could be born with cerebral palsy. All I wanted was to be able to give my baby a full life, free from the challenges I had faced as a child living with a disability.

The time I spent in the waiting room was the longest and hardest time I had ever experienced. I hoped and prayed Yessah and our baby were going to be okay.

I plugged my earplugs into my ears and listened to some of my favourite music on my iPhone in an attempt to keep calm. Then, like hearing the voice of a best friend you'd been separated from for nine long months, I heard the sound of a baby crying. It was a loud and high-pitched squeal and I instantly knew that was my baby.

My heart was filled with joy. I felt relieved, happy and excited and for those few moments my worries disappeared. At first, I wanted to run to be with Yessah and the baby, but Dad said we had to wait until we were called in. A nurse came out confirming it was our baby, a baby girl, and she was doing fine. She said Yessah had suffered some severe bleeding, losing one and a half litres of blood, but would also be fine.

What she didn't fully explain to us was that immediately after the baby was born, litres of blood began gushing from Yessah, as she held our baby on her chest for the first time. Medical alarms rang and several doctors rushed to Yessah's bedside to deal with the emergency that sent Yessah's temperature plummeting. The baby was taken away to a nearby hospital bassinet as Yessah lay frozen and shivering on the bed as a steady flow of blankets were laid over her in an attempt to warm her up. The blood loss had also sent Yessah's blood pressure to a dangerously low level, which we later discovered can be life threatening. But as her body warmed up slowly, and her blood pressure stabilised, a disaster was averted.

Back in the waiting room, I worried for Yessah, and was desperate to be united with my small family, but would have to wait. Dad called Mum to let her know the good news and she was thrilled, we all were, but I wanted to see them for myself, to know everything was going to be all right.

When the nurse finally allowed Dad and me into the birthing suite the first thing I saw was our baby girl with a mop of jet-black hair, just like Yessah's. I was grinning with pure joy. We had secretly known she was a girl and had chosen Shanaya as her name and she was beautiful. Yessah wasn't looking very well, however the nurse by her side assured me again she was going to be fine, and that's when I asked if I could hold my baby. She sat me in a chair not far from Yessah, who was being cared for by another nurse, but she could see from her bed that our baby was being placed carefully into my arms for her first cuddle with her daddy.

What a moment that was for me, holding my baby, the baby so many had told me I would never have. I kissed her forehead and immediately fell in love with the miniature mixture of the two of us. My thoughts were racing as I was really happy, excited, and relieved, but at the same time I was worried about the future. I wanted to give her the best life possible, but how was I going to provide for and take care of a baby girl? Again, dark thoughts about my disability returned, and doctors warning me about the risks of having a child with CP. I wasn't diagnosed until I was 13 months old, I wondered if there was a risk Shanaya could also have CP. I battled away these irrational, negative thoughts as I knew deep down that CP was not a genetic condition.

Yessah was feeling exhausted and not very well, but we were together, with our baby and our world was perfect.

Yessah and Shanaya stayed in the hospital for two nights and I visited as often as I could. The nurses came in regularly to check Yessah, which often included an internal examination. On each occasion they asked her whether she wanted me to leave the room, to which she always replied, "No, he is my partner." This disturbed Yessah and she wondered if mothers with non-disabled partners were given the same treatment.

When Shanaya and Yessah were ready to come home, Dad and I picked them up in his car which he had fitted with a baby seat. We sat in the front, while Yessah and Shanaya were securely strapped in the back seat, our first road trip with our baby. Mum was waiting for us at our place, where she had been busily preparing for our arrival and fresh flowers adorned the kitchen table as well as some gifts for Shanaya. Yessah carefully carried Shanaya into our unit taking delicate little steps as she navigated her way to our living room. As I watched Yessah, I could only dream of cradling Shanaya in my arms as I walked freely without my sticks, a task I would never be able to achieve.

It was an emotional meeting when Mum got to hold Shanaya for the first time. She looked just as relieved as I had felt when I first laid eyes on Shanaya, a perfect baby. Mum instantly saw the resemblance between Yessah and

Shanaya, and smiled as she teased, "Hayden, you didn't get a look-in, it's all Yessah", referring to her thick black hair.

Dad also had lots of cuddles with his granddaughter, his one and only grandchild, possibly the first baby he'd cradled in his arms since my birth 29 years earlier. We were so lucky to have my parents supporting us in those early days, and Dad had been instrumental in helping Yessah set up the cot, change table and nursery furniture, particularly when she decided to move everything into our bedroom from the nursery after arriving home from hospital. But it was only when my parents left us that day, that I realised the three of us were alone for the first time, our own little family.

It was a brand-new beginning, a new world with new smells, new sounds, new life! I had to pinch myself, I was so excited to be a father and to have my own child and a partner who loved me. I had proven all of the naysayers, the bullies, the doctors and the doubters wrong.

However, the early parenting days were tough as I was limited as to how I could assist Yessah physically, and she carried out most of the parenting duties. Yessah struggled with breast feeding Shanaya so she expressed her milk with a hand-held pump every few hours so that she had enough milk to feed her a bottle when she was hungry. And while I wanted desperately to help, my arms were not strong enough to hold up Shanaya's head while she fed from her bottle. It would be a several weeks before Shanaya's neck muscles were strong enough and Yessah felt comfortable for me to hold her to feed her. Even then a pillow was tucked above my arm and below Shanaya's head while she happily drank from her bottle. Yessah took on all of the baby duties, she changed her nappies, bathed her and put her into her bassinette when she was ready to sleep. Our precious baby was so fragile and tiny, I was very nervous about holding her in case she slipped through my less than perfect hands. Not being able to be a more involved father got me down at times as I felt helpless and wished I could be more useful. I was able to help out with cleaning around the house and by doing the weekly shop, but we also relied on Dad to give Yessah a break. He often came to our place in the mornings and helped me shower and change before I went to work at Woolworths, or he sometimes babysat Shanaya while Yessah had a nap.

But when Shanaya was five weeks old, the pressure began to take its toll on Yessah. She was often depressed and said she needed to get out of the house to meet people, to do something for herself. She got in touch with the aged care facility where she had worked as a food services assistant before Shanaya was born and was able to pick up three-hour shifts, twice a week. This gave her the freedom she needed, and she was happier. To ease the burden further, some nights I slept at my parents' house if I was working late, so that I didn't wake Yessah and Shanaya when I got home.

We were very lucky to have my parents who became an essential part of our support team helping us to raise our little girl. One of them would stay with me at our unit when Yessah went to work and sometimes both of them helped with bathing, feeding and changing Shanaya's nappies. They absolutely loved Shanaya and she brought them great happiness. As it unfortunately happens with some families, my Mum was estranged from my two older stepbrothers and their children, so Shanaya was the only grandchild Mum and Dad got to see, and they made the most of the precious time they were able to spend with her.

We enrolled Shanaya in a nearby creche where she was cared for on days Yessah and I were both working.

Dad usually came with me to drop her off and pick her up, and also to help me put her back into her car seat. When Shanaya was around eight weeks old she started smiling and gave us both the biggest smiles when we arrived at the crèche to collect her. This made me feel good because in the beginning I hated having to leave her with strangers. But she soon became a familiar face at the centre and even had her favourite carers. One of them was called Lucky, a delightful Indian woman whose cultural background shared many similarities with Yessah's and helped to create a special bond between them.

When Shanaya was several months old, my friend Brendan Faithful, who had been helping me out with a project I was working on, came with me to the crèche to drop Shanaya in for the day. The carer we left her with wasn't one of the usual workers and when we went to leave, she said to Shanaya, "Say goodbye to your dads!" Brendan and I looked at each other and realised the carer thought we were a gay couple dropping our daughter off for the day. We played along and both waved to Shanaya, laughing as we left the creche together.

Yessah and I ventured out like other young couples with our baby in her pram, but often we got stares from passers-by that parents who lived without obvious disabilities wouldn't get. Looks that rudely implied, "Are you sure she's yours?" however, nothing was ever verbalised, and I always just returned serve on the starers with a smile. There was no question between Yessah and me regarding Shanaya's parentage! The thick hair she had from birth grew into a curly mop of dark locks, just like Yessah's. Her skin took on a beautiful Mauritian olive tone and the shape of her face and eyes were identical to mine. She was our baby and we proudly showed her off to the world, despite their often-judgemental eyes.

As Shanaya grew bigger and more robust, I felt more confident handling her. When she graduated from sleeping in her bassinet to a cot next to our bed, I was able to confidently pick her up and move her quickly to our bed where we'd snuggle together under the doona, read books, play with toys and sometimes fall back to sleep in each other's arms.

For Shanaya's first birthday we had a small party at Mum and Dad's place. Mum cooked all the party food, and we celebrated our baby's first major milestone with a birthday cake and a small family celebration. She was our lucky charm, the baby who many told me I would never be able to have. I wanted Shanaya to have all of the opportunities I was given as a child. I wanted her to have good friends, to have a good education and follow her dreams. It was early days, but I thought she would share my love of sport because at the age of eighteen months, she already had good hand-eye co-ordination and could throw and catch a ball. I sometimes wondered how our relationship would develop as she got older and began to understand my disability. While I hung onto my dream of becoming an advocate and role model for other people living with disability, I also hoped I could be a role model for my daughter, and show her how to be a good person.

Chapter Eleven

2020 was a year like no other for the entire world and living with a disability during the coronavirus, or Covid-19, pandemic had its own, unique challenges. Covid-19 first emerged in Wuhan, China toward the end of 2019 when it began its steady spread across the globe like an octopus wrapping its tentacles around a beachball.

By February 2020 Australia's first case was reported in Victoria, after a traveller returning from Wuhan tested positive. Back then, nobody could have guessed the impact this highly contagious virus would have on their lives, work, education, sporting and social events, mental health and financial stability. Every continent was affected and within weeks some political leaders made swift decisions about how to slow the spread of the invisible enemy that was denying its most vulnerable victims the ability to breath by shutting down their lungs. Medical advisers recommended that politicians lock down entire populations in their homes to try to stop the spread of the virus. Either local government areas or whole states were restricted to staying in their homes and only leaving for essential reasons. During lockdowns, people had to work from home if they could, unless they were deemed to be essential workers or if they provided essential goods and services. School and university students had to adapt to remote learning, where they were given access to their schoolwork online, while the word 'zoom' was no longer considered a way to dart quickly from one place to another, but instead became the most common way to hold online visual work meetings, teacher-student conferences and social 'gatherings'.

Fortunately, as a supermarket employee, I was lucky enough to be deemed as an essential worker and I continued working through the pandemic at Woolies.

During the first Victorian Stage 3 lockdown in March, shopping for goods and services was one of the four reasons people were permitted to leave their homes. The other permitted reasons were for work or education (if you couldn't do it from home), to exercise or for care and compassionate reasons.

Once a government announced a lockdown was going to begin, usually within hours, customers converged on supermarkets everywhere to stock up on items like rice, flour, bread, spaghetti, hand sanitiser and toilet paper, fearing they would run out during the lockdown period which would last anywhere from three days to a few weeks, and on one occasion in Victoria was extended to five months.

The first time a lockdown was announced in Victoria, people began filling up their supermarket trolleys with packets of toilet paper. Yes, toilet paper! No one could really understand why, but for some reason this product became one of the most hotly sought-after items anyone could get their hands on. Busloads of shoppers from metropolitan areas where supermarkets ran short of essential items began heading to regional areas like Kyneton and stripped our supermarket shelves bare of anything they could grab, forcing Woolworths and other supermarket chains to put product limits on the groceries that were in the highest demand. So, instead of filling a trolley full of toilet rolls or packets of rice, shoppers were limited to one packet per customer.

Working on the checkout put me on the 'frontline' as I had to deal with the disgruntled customers when we ran out of any items. I was shocked by the amount of abuse I received during my shifts. Often, if customers missed out all together, they took their anger and frustrations out on me and the other checkout operators and verbally abused us. One male shopper singled me out and abused me for taking a job from a non-disabled person. He was in a rage and his behaviour was a direct result of the pandemic which had also resulted in thousands of people losing their jobs due to forced workplace closures during lockdowns.

Another shopper told me I was too slow and shouldn't be on the checkout. I was sad and angry to be on the receiving end of this abuse and wished I could have said to those angry customers that I, too, have a family to look after, bills to pay and need to work to put food on our table. But I was told not to bite back as Woolworth's policy maintains all customer complaints would be dealt with by management, so I had to keep my mouth shut. Except one

If I can, you can

occasion when I broke protocols and told a customer who was complaining about there being no toilet paper again. I told him there was plenty of sandpaper at Bunnings he could use, which he didn't like and walked away in a huff.

However, more often than not, people would come to my defence and deal with the rude and offensive customers. On one occasion, a well-known, high-profile lawyer who lived in the Macedon Ranges witnessed me being verbally abused at the checkout and followed the perpetrator and his equally rude partner out of the store where he gave them a piece of his mind. I couldn't hear what was being said but could see the lawyer and the couple head-to-head in a heated conversation outside the store's front window. I was grateful for those who stood up for me, including my manager who told me to ignore the criticism and reassured me I was a valued member of his staff and advised me that customers who were repeatedly abusive would be banned from the store.

During the pandemic I put myself in potential danger every time I went to work, possibly exposing myself to what had been revealed as a deadly virus, but I never passed on my fears or nervousness to my customers. I sanitised my hands after each customer and wiped down the register and workstation regularly. I tried to wear disposable gloves, but being a warm blooded person, they stuck uncomfortably to my sweaty palms. Before face masks became mandatory for everybody to wear, I decided to wear them while I was at work because, even before the pandemic, I always seemed to be the first one to catch a cold or flu that was going around. When I reminded shoppers to keep the 1.5 metre distance from each other, some acknowledged my requests, others simply ignored me or glared at me as if I didn't know what I was talking about.

I didn't see a lot of my regular, elderly customers who would usually choose my register, and I worried for them. Were they home alone with no human contact? Were they getting the essentials they needed to survive? I was relieved when Woolworths announced that the first opening hour of every weekday would be exclusively for seniors, pensioners, people with disabilities and those with health care cards. This dedicated hour for vulnerable shoppers who were missing out on essential items during the normally busy shopping hours guaranteed they could purchase what they needed, without the threat of hordes of people arriving to strip the supermarket bare, as they did earlier in the lockdown.

During the pandemic, I also worked from home for VicRoads, who had re-employed me in 2018, seven years after I lost my job there due to budget cuts. A year later in 2019 VicRoads and Public Transport Victoria merged to form part of the new Department of Transport (DoT). And while VicRoads continued as a licencing agency, DoT became my new employer. My work from home for DoT was as an administration assistant in the asset planning department. I spent three months Zooming with colleagues when meetings were required, but it wasn't the same as being in the office with colleagues. Previously, face-to-face breakfast meetings were always something I enjoyed with colleagues as it was our time to chat about our weekends, football and our families.

Working from home became the new normal for most Victorians during the state's longest lockdown, and we all learnt to deal with the inhouse distractions, like pets and children appearing out of nowhere during Zoom meetings! And while I loved being home and playing with Shanaya, our small unit wasn't ideal with Peppa Pig blaring in the background while I was trying to work. I often lost concentration and became frustrated when trying to compile data for my team. So, my parents came to the rescue again, offering to let me work from their house where I set up my computer in my old bedroom where the only singing I heard was from the birds in the backyard.

Shanaya was attending day care more regularly and as is the case with most young children building up their young immune systems, she picked up most germs or bugs that were being shared on communal toys smeared with communal snot. Before long, those germs were passed onto Yessah and me, resulting in all three of us being confined to our unit with Covid-like symptoms. During these days of the pandemic, if you had the slightest sniffle or tickle in your throat, you had to get a Covid test and isolate at home until you received a negative result from the health department, which would take anywhere between 24 hours and three or four days.

Yessah and I couldn't afford to be continually taking days off work so we decided that if Shanaya was unwell, Yessah would stay home with her and I would move into my parent's house until the coast was clear for me to return home. I spent weeks at a time living with my parents, separated from the two most important people in my life. Yessah, Shanaya and I FaceTimed every day, which gave me a strong sense of deja vu. Just as Yessah and I had FaceTimed in the early days of our romance, we were again speaking at our screens that were filled with our faces, but this time our gorgeous little girl joined in, waving at me from a few blocks away. It was very kind of my parents to take me in during this time, as they were in their 70's and were also very much at risk if they were to contract the virus. I relied heavily on them and they were an important part of our family dynamic.

There were many upsides to me staying with my parents. Like how Mum cooked my favourite lamb roast as only Mum can do, I got to spend time with my dog Bella, I binged on AFL footy games on Foxtel, and watched my old favourite kids' shows on Nickelodeon.

The pandemic had a detrimental effect on people's mental health, with news outlets reporting record numbers of people seeking help by calling suicide help lines. In September the Sydney Morning Herald reported that *Lifeline* had received 3,326 calls in one day, a thirty per cent increase on the same day the previous year. The lockdown isolation proved too much for many people to bare, many lost their jobs or had their incomes reduced, with welfare top-ups often not meeting weekly and monthly bills.

It became difficult for me to keep up with my physio and swimming during lockdown as the local swimming pool was closed and my physiotherapist, who usually accompanied me on my weekly swimming and running program, cancelled our sessions as he had just had a new baby and was not seeing any clients. This was also isolating, and not great for my mental health. I missed going to the local footy, volunteering and supporting the Kyneton Tigers. I missed not carrying out my duties as the official timekeeper and the interaction I usually had with other supporters, players and committee members. Not being able to go to Collingwood games was a strange feeling, too, and watching football on television with no crowds cheering and jeering in the stands was just weird. The AFL had been given permission by the health officials to continue playing games, providing TV entertainment to millions of supporters locked down in their homes. But, as there were no live spectators allowed at the grounds, fake crowd noises of clapping and cheering were pumped through the speaker systems at the football venues which could be heard throughout the television broadcasts.

However, the pandemic did have some positives and brought out the best in many people. Local builders gave up their time and the local hardware store donated tools and materials to build a COVID-19 respiratory screening centre at the hospital's old ambulance bay, enabling testing of the virus for anybody in the local community who had virus symptoms or had been at a COVID-19 exposure site. One of the local doctors' surgeries, Campaspe Family Practice, ran a competition for the town while in lockdown, with $500 prizes for the households who built the most impressive chicken house or vegetable garden. Stuck at home, people became creative and poured their energy into lockdown projects, giving them purpose and goals to achieve while being confined to their homes and properties.

Kyneton's Pizza and Wine Club offered free meals between 3:30 and 4pm for anyone 'doing it tough' in the local community. This was a collaboration between many of the town's businesses including the local butcher shop, Sizzlin' Sensations, Watts Fresh produce store, Kyneton Food Bank and Cobaw Community Health. Anybody needing a feed could drop in and pick up a meal for themselves, with additional meals costing just $5 each. It was acts of kindness like these that gave me hope during the pandemic, which was causing so much financial stress, anxiety and depression in our community.

Similarly, locked-down residents in cities all around the world who struggled with isolation took to their balconies to raise each other's spirits. Balcony singing became a nightly event in southern Italian cities before 'spreading' across Europe to Spain and Sweden (pardon the pun!).

Like supermarket workers, Yessah was also deemed to be an essential worker because of her job at the aged care facility as a food services assistant. This became scary during the month of July when the number of patients and staff at nursing homes across Victoria who were infected with COVID-19 was skyrocketing.

Every day that Yessah went to work she was greeted with a temperature gun, ensuring she didn't have a fever or any symptoms of the dreaded virus. She covered up with PPE (personal protective equipment), donning overalls, mask and face shield during her shifts where she served cups of tea and afternoon snacks to ageing, vulnerable residents.

There was fear in this facility that the virus would travel up the highway from Melbourne and spread across regional Victoria.

One employee who worked for several aged care facilities tested positive to COVID-19 at Yessah's workplace, but fortunately the infection didn't spread, and they were lucky enough to be spared the pain and suffering experienced in facilities where the virus was out of control. More than 800 Victorians, many elderly, lost their lives after COVID-19 spread across the state during 2020 following an outbreak sourced from the hotel quarantine system. In an attempt to stop the spread of the virus from returned travellers to Australia from overseas, they were required to quarantine in hotels of the government's choice for two weeks. Private security guards were hastily employed by the Victorian government to ensure everyone obeyed the rules and didn't spread the virus around, and also to ensure that anybody who returned a positive Covid-19 test whilst in quarantine was safely isolating during that 2-week period. But sadly, due to a lack of correctly followed infection control measures and the hastily assembled hotel quarantine system, an inquiry found that 768 deaths and more than 18 thousand cases of Covid-19 were caused as a direct result of the botched quarantine system.

Yessah and I both longed for a reprieve from the isolation, stress and worry we had dealt with through the pandemic. I longed to be able to take Yessah and Shanaya on a beach holiday to the Gold Coast, a holiday I had planned earlier in the year but had to cancel following Victoria's first Covid outbreak. I had visions of the three of us playing on the beach, swimming in the ocean and warming ourselves under the Queensland sun. But, like most others around the state, our holiday dreams were put on hold.

By the end of July, my three-year contract with the DoT came to an end, and while I was hoping the department would be able to keep me on, I knew that my employer, like many others, had taken an economic beating. By September 2020 Australia had fallen into an economic recession for the first time in three decades. The impact of the pandemic, its border closures, social distancing and lockdowns took its toll, and many businesses were forced to close. With our baby attending childcare, it was inevitable that Shanaya would pick up colds and coughs, as most babies and toddlers do in childcare settings. Therefore, we often had to keep Shanaya home forcing Yessah home, as well as having to take a few days off every time she herself had a sniffle. Working in the aged care sector meant Yessah was dealing directly with vulnerable elderly residents, and staff with any Covid symptoms were tested immediately and ordered to stay away until their Covid tests returned a negative result. Yessah was tested ten times for Covid during 2020 and thankfully she never tested positive but losing so many workdays was detrimental to our finances.

I still had my job at Woolworths, as well as my disability allowance, but our income wasn't meeting our weekly bills. Devastated by our financial situation, we had no choice but to dip into our savings that we had put away to one day buy a house. My wages covered the cost of our rent and food shopping, but the ongoing costs of nappies, baby formula, clothes and toys for Shanaya saw our house deposit dwindle rapidly. Our longing to one day own our own home took a further hit when the pandemic created a new breed of tree-changers, who chose to move to the country for more space and fresh air! This demand for housing in towns like ours pushed prices up, putting our dream country home out of reach.

As well as the tragic loss of life, the pandemic also killed off so many other social and sporting events, it closed openings and launches and capped numbers for those who could attend weddings and funerals. But one thing it didn't stop was local council elections.

I had been considering for a while how I could do more for my community and decided to nominate as a candidate in the Macedon Ranges Shire Local Government elections. I'd been fortunate enough to live in a great town with great people. Kyneton had been my home for 30 years and I planned on raising my daughter with Yessah in Kyneton. There were so many wonderful local businesses run by passionate people who also loved Kyneton and the Macedon Ranges. My mate, Jamie Gramberg, for example, owned the Cookie Crumbs café on Mollison Street and occasionally shouted me a coffee when I popped in, which was never expected but always accepted with great appreciation.

I wanted to be more involved and also to become an advocate for people with disabilities and the elderly by improving services for them in the Macedon Ranges. According to local government statistics, in 2016 there were 1,882 people living in the Macedon Ranges who needed help with their day-to-day lives because of a disability. Most were aged between 20 and 59, while the second largest group were aged over this. I believed my lived experiences provided me with the tools I needed to help make changes that could improve the lives of people living with disability in my local shire. Many were born with their disabilities like me, others developed a disability after illness, injury or accidents.

Within its boundaries, the Macedon Ranges was made up of nine towns, as well as several other smaller districts. Around 50,000 people lived in the Macedon Ranges, with a third of the population living in rural settings like farms and acreage.

The idea to run for council elections began as a joke in the DoT lunchroom earlier in the year, just weeks before working from home became the new normal. I was talking to a colleague about wanting to improve some basic services like footpaths in our area when he suggested I consider throwing my hat in the ring. I went home that night and began researching how I could make this possible. I later met with a former mayor who encouraged me to stand at the next election, but told me it would involve a lot of work and that there would be a lot of reading, council meetings once a month, as well as several other meetings with constituents and local businesses.

I thought to myself, I can do that, I can be a voice for others, I'm a familiar face in my community, one I think people, particularly the elderly, thought they could trust.

I discussed my ambitious ideas with Yessah who didn't warm to them immediately, as she was concerned about how much time I would need to commit to such a venture. But it was something I really wanted to do and she agreed to support me. At that point I decided to give it a go.

The only Australian politician I had heard of with cerebral palsy was Senator Jordon Steele-John who became the Australian Parliament's youngest senator at the age of 23. He had studied a Bachelor of Arts majoring in History and Politics at Sydney's Macquarie University before entering politics in 2017.

I was inspired by Senator Steele-John and hoped my candidacy could also be a positive influence for other people with ideas to step up and contribute to their local town. If they saw me having a go and fighting for my community, maybe others could be encouraged to do the same.

I announced my candidacy on Facebook in September 2020:

> Statement from Hayden
>
> Hi, I'm Hayden and I'm a West Ward candidate in the Macedon Ranges for 2020.
>
> I've lived in Kyneton and the Macedon Ranges all my life, and it has been good to me.
>
> Now it's my turn to do some good for my home.
>
> I want to be a good listener to all; I want to be a voice for disabled and elderly people in the Macedon Ranges and, more than that, I want to make life in the Macedon Ranges the best it can be. This means working with the local health authorities, local sports organisations and local businesses to achieve this.

A good start with this, I think, is being transparent about the key interests and concerns that I, and many other people living in the Macedon Ranges, have.

This is why I will publish a document very soon to publicly outline my Key Policies Platform, and make the key issues I wish to tackle if given the responsibility and privilege of serving as a councillor for the Macedon Ranges.

I hope I can count on your support and your votes.

One of the first areas I committed to giving attention to if elected would be the poor condition of some of the shire's footpaths. Some parts of Kyneton didn't have footpaths at all, forcing joggers, walkers, wheelchair users and parents with prams onto the road to complete their journey, while other streets that did have footpaths were in desperate need of upgrading. I had vivid memories of rolling my trike on more than one occasion when I rode from Mum and Dad's place to footy training. Large tree roots had risen up above the footpath, creating an uneven surface. But despite my repetitive emails to council seeking action, they remained unanswered.

My mate Brendan Faithful (you know, the one who was mistaken as my gay partner) took on the role of campaign manager and we had t-shirts screen printed reading HAYDEN WALSH WEST WARD 2020. The shirts were printed by another school friend, Eamonn Stanley, who started up a clothing company called Sir Harold Apparel, based on a fictional character he invented with a group of mates in 2008. Sir Harold was considered a small-town cult hero with his own website and clothing range. His distinct face, complete with moustache and spectacles, could be found printed on t-shirts, hoodies, tracksuit pants and even face masks! Ever the entrepreneur, Eamonn even launched his own Sir Harold Apparel Tokyo Olympics range ahead of the 2021 Games, branding his sportswear TEAM SHA. He described his team as the world underdogs, his online shoutout for supporters included one prerequisite, *'If you're shit, you're perfect'*! Jokes aside though, Eamonn is a true community warrior and has supported fundraising efforts throughout the town, including one for the KFNC when they were really struggling financially some years back.

So, back on the campaign trail, I physically started doorknocking local businesses in the three main streets of Kyneton—Piper Street, Mollison Street and High Street— keen to get to know the local traders and learn how my campaign could help them, as well as vying for their vote at the next council election!

Piper Street was considered one of the most popular restaurant districts in regional Victoria. The historic facades of buildings, including bluestone bricks and antique windows, created an idyllic destination for city-dwellers keen for a rural getaway. But the cobblestone footpaths were not so great for people with mobility issues and I made a note to add that to the list of issues to be addressed by council!

The pandemic had a big impact on Piper Street, just as it had on all tourist destinations. The usually bustling shopping strips were deserted, except for the loyal locals desperately trying to keep their favourite cafes and pubs afloat by purchasing take away coffees and meals. Piper Street was home to restaurants, cafes, antiques stores, art galleries, clothing shops, bakeries, produce stores and different types of accommodation. I wanted my campaign to highlight why new businesses should come to Kyneton, just one hour from Australia's second largest capital city.

I campaigned on Facebook and in the local newspaper and received lots of good feedback from residents. However, not all of the local constituents were on my side. Some presumed I was aligned with the Labor Party because I had 'liked' a post on the official Facebook page of Victorian Premier Daniel Andrews, who was 'on the nose' with a lot of Victorians following the failed hotel quarantine debacle. Others were downright cruel. One man wrote on my Facebook page that I lacked the intensity needed to follow through with my plans. Another wrote that I didn't have the intellectual ability required to be a councillor. Obviously, none of them knew my academic history! I understood being a public figure would require having a thick skin, and mine had grown thick enough over the years of living with a disability to deal with these offensive keyboard warriors.

The elections were held in October with votes counted and results announced in early November. I didn't win, but 752 people voted for me, that's 7.21% of the primary vote. I was disappointed I didn't win, but pleased with myself for having a go. Yessah was also proud of me, but she conceded she was relieved when I wasn't victorious, as she wanted me to be free to spend as much time as possible with her and Shanaya.

By December 2020, we prepared for Christmas with Shanaya's presents wrapped and hidden in our bedroom cupboard. I was rostered to work a Christmas Eve shift at Woolworths from 4 PM until 9 PM. It was one of those nights I decided to stay at my parent's house, so that I didn't disturb Shanaya and Yessah who planned on going to bed early. We'd arranged for Yessah to wake me in the morning with a phone call when Shanaya woke up, and I would return home to see her open her Christmas presents. What I didn't know was it took Yessah several hours to assemble a toy kitchen that Santa had given her for Christmas, while I slept soundly at my parent's place. By six AM on Christmas morning, Shanaya was up and running around the unit desperate to open her presents under our first real Christmas tree. But when Yessah rang me, I was out to it, and barely made any sense, telling her to go ahead with the present opening without me, before I fell back into a deep sleep for another couple of hours. When I finally woke and drove home, I was shattered I had missed out on Shanaya's special Christmas morning of opening presents and seeing if the reindeer had eaten the carrots and drunk the beer that had been left out for them.

Yessah had tried, but there was no way she was going to stop our 21-month-old from her early morning present opening. While devastated, I was used to the way my medication had dictated my mornings since my bipolar diagnosis 13 years earlier. If I ever considered not taking my meds so that I could wake earlier or not miss events like Christmas and birthdays, I only had to recall the dreadful consequences that landed me in a psychiatric ward at 17 years of age. That was more than enough to make me swallow the essential little pills.

I spent the afternoon with Shanaya, pretending to cook food in her new toy kitchen before my parents joined us for dinner at our unit. Mum roasted a chicken and brought it with her when she and Dad arrived, as well as the Woolworths pavlova she decorated for dessert. Yessah roasted a lamb and vegetables, as well as making a salad for our Christmas feast. It was a small family celebration, but we were all so grateful to be spending precious time together, following a year that saw so many people experience loss and grief on a scale never seen before.

2020 had been a big year, one we had endured and survived and by New Year's Eve we were happy to bid it farewell. Yessah and I felt we had got through one of the toughest years of our lives. We managed to hold down our jobs, (except for the DoT position), we all avoided contracting the virus and I ran for council. My involvement in the council elections gave me the confidence to consider how else I could make a difference in my community, and I already had my sights set on a new project for 2021, and was excited to hopefully see it come to fruition.

Chapter Twelve

As I stood on the podium at the Williamstown Football Club social rooms, I looked down to the closest table, table nine, and saw the beaming faces of Yessah with Shanaya on her lap, and my parents, all clapping their hands along with hundreds of other guests at the pre-match President's lunch. I had a flashback to my secondary school visits from Jim Asimakopoulos sharing his cerebral palsy story, and my aspirations to one day do the same. Fast forward almost two decades and there I was telling the Hayden Walsh cerebral palsy story to a captive audience.

It was the Williamstown Football Club's dedicated 'Inclusion Round' where the Williamstown Seagulls' all-abilities side played a game against the Ballarat Bulldogs, a curtain-raiser to the scheduled VFL match between Williamstown and Geelong.

I was invited to tell my story as a footballer with a disability, and was interviewed by the Williamstown CEO, Jason Reddick. It was a great feeling having an attentive crowd who even laughed at my jokes. Jason asked me how my team was going in the competition, and tongue-in-cheek I replied, "We've been very competitive..." (which is usually code for not very good), "...and we're on the bottom of the ladder," which the crowd found very funny as I delivered my response with a wry smile. The laughter reached another level when Jason then told me I sounded like Port Melbourne VFL coach, Gary Ayres, whose team had been having a bad year too. "I know Gary Ayres well,"

I quipped. The crowd was loving the banter, and Jason retorted, "Don't tell him I said that!"

Jason had been given the heads-up about my many media appearances over the years and told the audience I had a reputation as 'dial a quote'. He joked, "I've heard you're in the media every second day, Hayden," to which I replied, "Yeah, most of the time," and the crowd just lost it, showing their appreciation of our comedic toing and froing with a huge round of applause. Feeling very happy with my performance, I slowly walked down the podium steps with my sticks and joined my family at the table.

The audience was made up of a combination of Williamstown Football Club members and organisers of the Victorian Football Integration Development Association (FIDA), which ran the all-abilities football competition. Following my speech, several people came to my table and shook my hand, including FIDA representatives and all-abilities players from other FIDA teams. My contribution to the luncheon had been a success and I was proud of myself. Yessah told me she was proud of me too. It was the first time she had heard me speak publicly, and was amazed and excited by how well I had been received by the audience.

It was 2021 and several weeks into the football season, which had marked my long-awaited return to playing footy for the Kyneton Football Netball Club.

Eighteen years earlier I had reluctantly shed my South Kyneton footy jumper when my parents decided that the game was too dangerous for me to play with the Under 13 boys.

But I never gave up on the hope that one day I would again be able to pull on the black and yellow guernsey and run onto the Kyneton Showgrounds oval as a Kyneton Tiger.

I'd spent the early part of 2021 working with the footy club to include a new team made up of all-abilities players with physical and intellectual disabilities into the Victorian FIDA League. The Covid-19 pandemic had settled down and the number of people returning positive tests in Victoria reduced to zero, except for overseas travellers who were quarantining in hotels. Sporting clubs were gearing up for a return to having crowds at games and players looked forward to competing in front of loyal supporters after a full season of no football the previous year.

The Bendigo Suns FIDA team I'd previously played for involved traveling every weekend to clubs as far north as the New South Wales border, three hours north of Kyneton.

So, having a local FIDA club in Kyneton would reduce the travel time for players like myself by several hours every weekend. I happily began wearing my media hat again, becoming the face of Kyneton's new FIDA program, appearing in local newspapers and television stories promoting a tryout day for people interested in joining the team. Given the number of people living with disabilities in the Macedon Ranges, as well as disability services provided through Cobaw Community Health and Windarring, I was confident we would have enough girls and boys aged over 14, as well as women and men, to fill the team. I contacted the electoral office of my local member of parliament, the Honourable Mary-Anne Thomas, requesting that she mention the new Kyneton FIDA team to parliament. She did this within weeks and then posted the video of herself speaking about the FIDA team on her Facebook page. I was hoping that by spreading the word more people with disabilities would want to join the team. Mary-Anne personally replied to me and arranged a coffee catch-up at the local Homegrown Café in Kyneton where we chatted about the FIDA competition and she asked me ways I thought she could assist people with disabilities in the Macedon Ranges. She also congratulated me on my recent local government campaign to become a councillor, even though I wasn't elected.

My involvement with FIDA began opening doors in 2021 that I couldn't have imagined. After Channel 9 featured me in a television news story promoting the new team, I was contacted by the *Dylan Alcott Foundation* and asked if I would be interested in doing some promotional work for them. Never one to miss an opportunity, I jumped at the chance to get my face out there as a disability advocate and accepted the offer. The foundation was working on a project creating advertisements for the 'SPORT4ALL' campaign, with the theme of inclusivity at the forefront, and my first photoshoot was at a warehouse in Collingwood. It was the middle of February and COVID restrictions were starting to relax, meaning facemasks were no longer required. I felt very special and I had my hair and makeup done by a professional stylist. Better late than never, I'd thought; it had only taken nineteen years to get the modelling work I was hoping for when I was an eleven-year-old Auskicker!

The photoshoot went for about four hours and during that time I was photographed throwing and catching a football with other people with disabilities, including a comedian, a swimmer and another FIDA footballer and friend, Zander. The SPORT4ALL campaign, funded by the federal government, aimed to raise awareness in the community that people with disabilities can be involved in their local sporting clubs and enjoy the competitive and social environment just as much as any other sportspeople.

A couple of weeks later I was again required for the same campaign with another four-hour commitment. This time I was videoed kicking a footy with a blind footy player at Glen Iris in Melbourne's south east. Camera operators filmed us from the ground using a traditional camera, and then from above using a drone. It was a very exciting day and I felt fantastic being able to show that sportspeople with disability wanted to be involved in sporting clubs, and didn't want to be left behind.

My next assignment for the foundation attracted a high level of media interest when Federal Treasurer Josh Frydenberg and Senator Anne Ruston launched the Morrison Government's support for 'Get Skilled Access', programs which also aimed to increase sport participation for people with disability and to build disability awareness and education in hospitals. I was filmed playing tennis with Dylan Alcott and Josh Frydenberg at the launch which was at the Camberwell Tennis Club, and the stories were aired on all the major television networks that night. I must have been quite impressive because soon after that job the Dylan Alcott Foundation signed me up as a consultant, advising that they would call upon me to share my sporting stories at future events. This work with the Dylan Alcott Foundation was always welcome, as were the extra funds deposited into our bank account.

Within months of me becoming a consultant with the Foundation, Dylan played his final Grand Slam match at

the Australian Open in January 2022, after announcing his retirement from tennis. He was runner-up in the quad singles championship, but took the opportunity during his after-match speech to call for more prize money for wheelchair tennis tournaments. Thirty-six hours earlier, Alcott had flown to Canberra where he was awarded the honour of being named the 2022 Australian of the Year. During his emotional and at times humorous speech, Alcott described himself as a proud man with a disability. He told the audience that he didn't think he had a chance of taking out the award, but joked that when he saw the ramp going up to the stage, he felt he was in with a chance. He went on to highlight the high unemployment rate for people living with disabilities, but quipped, "we are not just ready to work, we are ready to take your jobs... we are coming!" I feel so lucky to have Dylan as an advocate for the disability sector and role model and can't wait to see what he can achieve in 2022. I am thrilled to be involved with the Dylan Alcott Foundation, and hope my contribution will help in some way to improve representation for people with disabilities in sport, the workplace and their communities.

The media exposure around the Kyneton FIDA team made me an easy go-to for local journalists wanting comments relating to the disability sector, which explained the dial-a-quote gag at the Williamstown luncheon. In May I was contacted by a Channel 9 News journalist from Bendigo and asked if I would comment on the proposed changes to the way the NDIS assessments were made. Since its inception in 2013, the NDIS changed the way funding was distributed to people with disabilities for the better.

In her emotional speech to Federal Parliament on 15th May, 2013, then Prime Minister Julia Gillard commended the new NDIS Bill to the house: "*In years to come, Disability Care Australia will ensure... young people with disability will have the security and dignity every Australian deserves. The idea of a national disability insurance scheme has found a place in our nation's hearts, we gave it a place in our nation's laws, now we inscribe it in our nation's finances.*"

My Channel 9 interview was filmed at the local *Monsieur Pierre* café, the place Yessah loved so much because of its French influence, and I was asked about the importance of my NDIS funding and why I needed it. I told the reporter it helped ensure I had important physiotherapy sessions and consultations with my surgeon who could check on how my hips and legs were travelling. Without this ongoing monitoring, I could easily have fallen into bad habits which could have been detrimental to my mobility and pain management. Hopefully, my inclusion in news stories like that one shone a light on how people with disabilities felt in real life, rather than simply listening to other people who spoke on our behalf.

I was proud of the work I was doing to improve the lives of people with disabilities, it was a personal goal of mine to continue to develop this type of advocacy.

One of the biggest highlights of the year came when I finally got to run out onto the Kyneton Showground oval wearing the mighty Kyneton Tigers' yellow and black guernsey. It was the first time I'd been able to play for my club since I was thirteen years old, playing in the Under 13's. Fast forward eighteen years and at the age of thirty-one I led my own all-abilities Tiger's team onto the oval in front of a hometown crowd of around 1,000 people. It was a huge buzz for all of the men and women who had come together and trained for weeks ahead of the big day. I felt incredibly proud of the preparation I had done with the Kyneton Football Netball Club in the previous months to get the FIDA team up and running.

It was a Saturday afternoon and the opening round of the Bendigo Football Netball League competition. Supporters had been kept away from their beloved game for over a year because of the COVID-19 pandemic and were eager to watch some local footy and netball again.

The netballers played their games on the court adjacent to the football oval and also drew a big crowd of fans keen for the netballers' return to the court. A coffee van helped fuel the spectators' energy levels while warming their freezing hands, and security guards ensured that no one tried to sneak in their own alcohol, which had to be bought from either the outdoor marquee or the bar inside the club's social rooms.

The netball games kicked off the day and the first football match was the under 18's game at midday. Our FIDA game wasn't an official home and away game as our season was due to begin the following week. So, we instead scheduled a practice match with Rupertswood, who travelled from Sunbury for the 2pm start.

Our game had been deliberately scheduled before the reserves' and senior footballers' games, which sent a strong signal to the entire community of the KFNC's commitment to inclusivity. So, by the time our game was due to start, it felt like the whole town was gathered around the ground, waiting for our two sides to battle it out, limps, walking sticks, wheelchairs and all.

Before the game Heath Davidson, Paralympian, quad wheelchair champion and doubles partner of Dylan Alcott, gave our team a pep talk in the change rooms, revving us up to get out there and have some fun. Heath also tossed the coin in the middle of the oval to determine which team would have first choice of kicking direction to start the game.

I can vividly remember my name being chanted by Kyneton spectators as I ran out of the clubrooms and approached the gates onto the ground. It was an exhilarating and exciting moment; one I will never forget.

However there was one moment that almost ruined my day when some well-intentioned supporters grabbed hold of my arms to help me onto the ground, when all I really wanted to do was run out on my own two feet, albeit slower than the other players. I'm sure they thought they were doing the right thing, but I knew that I was perfectly capable of getting myself onto the oval unassisted, just as

I had done in every game I had played before that one. I felt determined from that moment that if anyone ever tried to 'help' me again, I'd make sure that I'd politely let them know that I can do it by myself.

Through connections with the AFL's Richmond Tigers, the KFNC ensured it would be a special day for its FIDA team with a special banner welcoming the players onto the Kyneton Showgrounds oval for their first hit out. A local bloke known as Woodend Trout arranged through his involvement with the Richmond cheer squad for the materials for the banner to be shared with our club. Trout then helped a small army of Kyneton Tiger Juniors, the President Hayden Evans and Junior Director Daniel Murray cut and tape huge amounts of yellow and black crepe paper until their project was complete. We felt like superstars seeing the magnificent banner with the words emblazoned, "IF I CAN TAKE THIS STEP TODAY, I CAN TAKE ANY STEP TOMORROW."

Once on the ground I led our team through a guard of honour formed by the Under 18 boys who had just finished their game. This was a really meaningful and special moment and a touching mark of respect for us. As we got closer to the glorious banner, the Rupertswood players joined our team and we all ran through it together as a united group. Unfortunately, multiple layers of sticky tape made it difficult for me to break through the banner's material so our coach, Joel Bertoncini, also my Woolworths mate, had to cut the tape so I could run through it!

People I knew well in the crowd told me later that they had tears rolling down their cheeks throughout the pre-game build up, and I wasn't far off it myself.

The game was played in great spirits with the umpire ensuring players from both sides got to have a kick and some of us were even lucky enough to score a goal! There was no doubt I was the crowd favourite, and I could hear the roar from the crowd when I kicked the ball off the ground, and it dribbled through the centre posts for a goal. It reminded me of the cheer I got at Princes Park when I kicked that Auskick goal over a decade earlier.

It was a tough game, and my match fitness probably wasn't up to scratch, which caused me to cramp up towards the end of the last quarter. I had a sense of deja vu when a strong gust of wind pushed me to the ground, reminding me of my school days at Sacred Heart. I bet the boys got a good laugh out of that one, too!

I had a couple of hours to recover from my game, talking to supporters while watching the reserves play, before taking up my usual position in the timekeepers' box for the senior men's game. Settling into the redbrick timekeepers' box, I switched on the heater to warm up my feet and legs that were still aching from playing four quarters of football. I had a few quiet moments to reflect on how lucky and proud I was to be part of the Kyneton Football Netball Club, which had gone to great efforts to ensure the all-abilities team was included in its round one blockbuster, in such a special way.

To cap it off, the following Tuesday a full-page photo of our teams running through the banner was featured on the front page of the local newspaper, the *Midland Express*, along with the heading, 'INSPIRATIONAL'. There was also a photo of me in the sports pages holding the footy during the game with the caption, "Club stalwart Hayden Walsh was a crowd favourite." It was a very special day and one I will always cherish.

While football provided so many wonderful experiences and opportunities for me in 2021, the same couldn't be said for my idol, Nathan Buckley. Unrest had been growing within the Collingwood Football Club following the team's poor performance, with only three wins by round twelve in the home and away season. Then, under growing pressure to resign as coach, Nathan announced that Collingwood's round 13 game against the Melbourne Football Club would be his last at the helm for the Magpies. I was devastated for Nathan and felt he had been treated badly by the club he had played 260 games for, and coached at for ten years.

As I watched the match from home the following Monday afternoon, tears of sadness ran down my cheeks when the Magpies were victorious, defeating ladder-leaders Melbourne by 17 points at the Sydney Cricket Ground. In a sign of gratitude, Collingwood players embraced Nathan after the game, many of them in tears, before both sides formed a guard of honour for him to walk through, exiting the SCG to a standing ovation from the crowd of sixteen-and-a-half thousand people. I was happy Collingwood had taken the win, but sad Nathan would no longer be part of the club, and I wondered if there would be any opportunities for our paths to ever cross again.

Employment prospects continued to improve in 2021 following my successful job application with the John Holland Construction Group in Melbourne. I was offered work one day a week as an administrative assistant where I entered data into spreadsheets and typed up work orders for the procurement department. I began to feel that 2021 was a turning point in my life; good things were happening in waves, and I was determined to catch them like a dedicated surfer, only my board was my sticks, and my ocean was my life.

Our little girl, Shanaya, turned two in March and she was no longer the fragile newborn I once feared would slip through my crooked fingers. Her dark hair had grown longer and curlier and her dark eyes grew more curious every day. She'd grown into a robust toddler who I rolled around with on the floor and threw a ball to in our small backyard. Having a partner and child made my conviction to staying as fit and as strong as possible, and keeping my weight under control even more of a priority. My body had been through so many operations, treatments and procedures to get me on my feet and walking, and that's how I wanted my life to continue. I would need to work hard to stay mobile and I simply refused to see myself ever relying on a wheelchair again.

Yessah and I continue to dream of owning our own home, with a big kitchen so she can cook her favourite Mauritian dishes, and a big bathroom with a bath for me to relieve my aching muscles after a long day at work. We picture Shanaya swimming in our very own backyard pool, hopefully with a younger brother or sister. And when we dare to dream even further, we see our little family splashing around in the shallows at the beach, just a short walk from our modest beach house.

Acknowledgements

There are many people who I would like to thank for their contributions to 'If I can, you can'. The book would not have come to life if Hayden had not said "yes" when I asked him if I could write his biography. We spent many, many hours together where Hayden told me his life-story in great depth. Thank-you for trusting me and giving me the opportunity to share your story Hayden, it has been an absolute pleasure. Thank you for your honesty and vulnerability, which enabled me, through your voice, to provide your first-hand account of a person living with a disability, including the endeavours, achievements and challenges you have experienced along your journey so far. I hope this book will assist in providing more opportunities for you to expand your endeavours to advocate on behalf of others, also living with disabilities.

Thank you to Hayden's partner Yessah, his extended family and friends, former teachers, work colleagues and sporting associates who I interviewed for the book. There are too many to name, but all of them provided personal insights into their relationships with Hayden and their recollections have enabled Hayden's story to be told.

Thank you to Libby Thompson from "The Write Word", who generously gave her time to edit chapters, ask questions and flesh out themes that needed exploring. The final product is a testament to Libby's editing skills. Thank you to Jim McIlwain and Tracey Spicer, AM for providing invaluable contributions and feedback.

Thank you to stylist Ben Amery, Regan Kennedy from Regan K makeup and Carl Morris for providing their time and expertise for photoshoots with Hayden, Yessah and Shanaya. Thank you to Terese and Troy Parsons for facilitating a photo shoot at their home.

Thank you to Nathan Buckley, Stephen Rielly from the Collingwood Football Club, and Rob Waters from Channel Ten for your contributions.

Thank you to my great girlfriends and Book Club who have supported me while I procrastinated for years about writing a book.

Thank you to the Kyneton Football Netball Club and Aesop's Attic Bookshop in Kyneton for their ongoing support.

And to my family, my amazing Mum, sisters and brother who have supported and encouraged me on my journey. To my wonderful husband Martin and sons, Max, Tommy, Ned and Jack, I could not have achieved my goal without your constant support.

Finally, a huge thank you to Howard Firkin of in case of emergency press, for his amazing generosity, for having confidence in me as a writer and teaching me about the world of short run publishing.

About the Author

Karen O'Sullivan is a National Award-winning journalist who worked in the Melbourne media for 28 years. Karen began her journalism career at Radio 3AW, before joining Channel 10. Most recently Karen spent 13 years as the 7 Network's multiple award-winning Health Reporter.

Karen won the National Luminous Award for Excellence in Oncology reporting three times, in 2006, 2011 and 2014. Karen was the winner of the 2013 Australia and New Zealand Mental Health Media Award and received a High Commendation in the Victorian Quill Awards in 2011.

Karen lives on a sheep farm with her husband in country Victoria, they have four sons. Karen is committed to working within the Kyneton community where she is a Director on the Board of Central Highlands Rural Health, a former Committee member of the Kyneton and Hanging Rock Race Club and a former President of the Kyneton Football Netball Club, the organisation's first female President in its 150 year history.

Karen's website is:
www.koms.com.au

www.ingramcontent.com/pod-product-compliance
Lightning Source LLC
Chambersburg PA
CBHW022056290426
44109CB00014B/1115